Author

Chad Thilborger
www.awholeheap.com

Design

Isaiah Chavez

Photography

Jason Leidy
Middle River Arts Photography,
http://www.middleriverarts.com/

Whole Heap

DEDICATION

The hardest thing for me to write. I dedicate this book to my entire family.
I could never ever have done this without my family, especially Mom, Jeff
and Kevin. From Maw Maw to Nanny and Mom I learned to love food. Frank
has been a critical part of the development of this book and his inspiration,
courage, and most importantly patience have helped to make this dream a
reality. The Love and support of so many friends and family have made cooking
and food more meaningful to me. To all of you, I LOVE you and appreciate all
you do for me.

With all of this love and inspiration, I dedicate this book to those I love and
those who have and continue to love me!

Now bottom line, It's a Whole Heap, so Dig In!!!

Enjoy & Savor the flavors of Home!

Why I Did This!

My family is obsessed with food. At breakfast we talk about what we are going to have for lunch. At lunch…. Well you get the picture. You might think that this is because we have nothing to say to each other or that we are trying to avoid sensitive topics. Nothing could be further from the truth. Getting a rise out of each other is one of my family's favorite hobbies. The real reason we talk about food is that we have so many memories of how homemade food made family gatherings and everyday meals more enjoyable. To be completely honest, my family never had a lot of money. But those folks who took the extra time, thought and care to prepare homemade food are undeniably precious to me.

My mom and I share a love of cooking. We both love to take family's recipes and add our secret twists to make them "ours". To this day, cooking is a way for us to express originality, and more importantly, to bring together the people that mean the most to us and cook for them. I believe that serving home cooked food makes everyday moments more special and it shows people that you care about them.

We inherited this from her mother, who I called Maw Maw, and she undoubtedly did the same with hers. This book is full of her recipes and my memories of cooking with her. I have also included recipes from friends and other members of my family. My selection criteria for which to include was simple –did I enjoy making and eating it and did I like to serve it to my guests.

Initially, I never intended to write a cookbook. One afternoon when I was cleaning out a closet, I stumbled upon an old box. There was an old drawing inside that inspired me to start compiling all these old family recipes before we lost them. When I opened the box, I found a drawing my Maw Maw made for me. And my Maw Maw, bless her heart never got the level of education she deserved. This drawing was a pictorial recipe for her biscuits which she made every Sunday we visited. I remember how much love she put into her cooking; how her house smelled with warm biscuits coming from the oven. I started remembering about how she taught me some of her easier recipes and how I could change them up and make them even more special. This got me thinking about other loving people in my life like my Mom and Aunt Nanny Annie and those who have since passed like Maw, Uncle Pat, Dad, Paw, and Miss Diane who shared their love of cooking. I got in touch with friends, my family and the families of those who had passed and asked for the recipes. It some way collecting and publishing the recipes and their stories was a way to thank them and to ensure that they were never lost and hopefully enjoyed by many, many more people.

However, during the process, I soon realized that there were no recipes for some of my favorite foods. My mom simply learned from watching and cooking with Maw Maw. I had to include these recipes. So early this summer, I flew home to New Orleans to spend time with mom. For 5 days, we shopped, chopped, fried, fricasseed and baked the foods from my childhood. Mom recounted some of her favorite memories when she got to prepare and serve them. I diligently wrote down the directions and her stories.

In essence, this isn't just a cookbook. It really is my Food Memoir. I also hope it will inspire more folks to make everyday moments a little more special by preparing home cooked food. But I also want folks to express their own tastes and preferences. That's why on many pages there is a space for you to write down how you made this recipe your own and perhaps some information about the moment that you served it. In the future, you can share it with your family and hopefully make those recipes part of your family's traditions and heritage.

Now you should know that I am no trained chef. I have never been to culinary school. And while my knife skills are above average, they will never mesmerize people who watch me prep a kitchen. But fortunately, I have had more culinary successes than failures. I started with these family recipes. I added my own little touches and ingredients to make them unique. And I have included those touches in my recipes. I hope your family will enjoy them as much as mine.

Finally, I hope that this memoir and culinary journey brings you a whole heap of smiles. It certainly does this for me when I got to share my stories and recipes with you.

Whole Heap

Table of Contents

SOUPS

ENTREES AND SIDES

DESSERTS

My Philosophy

As a 6'4" man from New Orleans with roots deep in the heart of Cajun Country, with a booming voice and even bigger laugh, people always describe me as "larger than life". But to family and friends who really know me, it has little to do with my size and much more to do with how I live my life. Essentially, I believe that you get a Whole Heap more out of life when you add more spice, more color, or even a tad more effort into the everyday things to make life more fun, more meaningful and ultimately more rewarding. My partner often tells a story about me and baked beans, which sums it all up. You see, I have never met a can of baked beans I won't doctor. I add a little of this and a little of that along with a splash of a bit more and there ya have it. It takes all of two minutes to add everything. But I know my guests will enjoy them more and feel even more special because I have made an extra effort to make it extra special. And when I do things like this, it strengthens the connections and relationships I have. It Makes the Moment Momentous!

That's the idea behind Whole Heap. Whole Heap helps everyone make everything a bit better, a dab more dynamic, more emotional and of course a Whole Heap of special. We don't just give you ideas, we tell you stories that show ya'll how to serve up a Whole Heap of life by having more fun, being more colorful, stretching your creativity, adding more spice, savoring more sweetness, giving back a little more and making it ALL more meaningful. Here at Whole Heap, my attitude about life is, "Dig in".

What's the Point?

There are thousands and thousands of cookbooks, websites and food ideas and philosophies out there. Over the last several years it has even become hip to be Southern. The bottom line for me is that food and how we serve it tells a story. Food connects us those around us as well as to the events that happen within our lives. I can remember Holidays, weddings funeral, graduations, birthdays and so many regular old weekends. Why are they important? They all shaped me. The people around us shape us. The food we share shapes us. Food touches every one of our senses it lingers in our mind and stirs the memories. To this day when I smell glazed donuts I think of sitting at a donut counter it my dad or sitting in a kitchenette at a funeral home or sneaking around the corner to buy a few without anyone at home knowing. Let's all take the journey together and make food together and make memories that last and those who we love smile.

Lagniappe

I LOVE Louisiana cooking. But as you can see from the photos in my cookbook, there is a Whole Heap beige and brown going on. With roux and rice, gumbos and dressings, crawfish and sausage, it isn't the most colorful food. I could always add fresh flowers. But when I entertain, I usually serve family style with heaping platters of food. So with flowers, there never seems to be enough room on the table for the food and I don't want a big bouquet blocking my view of my guests. So whenever I entertain friends and family, I try and do something a little special with the table. At first, I would tie the napkins with a sprig of rosemary or oregano from my garden. And I still do that. But as you might suspect, my Whole Heap philosophy found its way into not only in my cooking, but also how I set a table and decorate my home. I have to admit, I am almost as happy when friends compliment me on the table as I am when they comment on the food.

As you also might have guessed, I get that from my mom. A few years ago, I was visiting my mom and stepdad. After a few meals mom took off the table cloth and put a fresh one down, even though the other one was still clean. When I asked her why she did that, she said that we had eaten on that one a couple of times and she wanted to have something different and make the table look nice. I appreciated the gesture but didn't think much more about it.

The very next day mom and I were shopping in some small shops in Covington, a town about 10 miles north of New Orleans. It is a quaint riverfront town full of antique shops and mom and pop stores. We went into a small store owned and run by an elderly couple that was stocked to the rafters with limited run fabrics. There were rich brocades, colorful silks and soft velvets. And then it hit me. This is what Whole Heap was missing; affordable table linens and accessories that give people the flexibility to change up a table runner, napkins or place mats as well as decorative pillows for their home without overspending. So I began to buy fabric, a lot of limited run fabrics.

At first, I made pillows and table linens for my home. My friends commented on how beautiful they were and had never seen anything like them in stores. So I started making some of these items as gifts. They told me that their guests reacted the same way. And that's how my line of Whole Heap table linens and home furnishings got started.

If you look closely at the pictures in this cookbook, you will notice that many of the pictures show plates or serving dishes sitting atop some of my fabrics. I constantly refresh the selection as these limited fabric runs, run out. But you can count on one thing, I will always have new fabrics for my

Whole Heap line. To see what is now available, just visit www.awholeheap.com.

Now I have a warning for you, when you visit the website, you will not find finished pillows, place mats and table runners for sale. What you will find are photos of fabrics and how much of it is available. We will tell you how much yardage you need for each of them. After all, one person may want pillows while another might think the fabric is perfect for the table. This way you decide how to make your home a whole heap more special.

I was asked why I don't make thousands upon thousands and sell them to stores. Well this defeats the purpose of short runs and special items, but most importantly, helping my clients find something more unique. So, I am happy to produce the items that you want in the fabric you want especially for you.

I have also been asked why table linens and pillow covers, well that's easy, nothing can change the look of a room faster than a few pops of color or a uniquely designed piece of fabric. I have kept all the sizes standard so it is easy for you to change out one pillow cover for another in order to change up the look of a room for a season, special occasion or just to make a unique change. So enjoy these and have a Whole Heap of fun with this line.

Brunch or Breakfast Gatherings

In true N'awlins and Cajun fashion, I am social. I love to have people over even when folks come over with a hangover from hell. With the right food, the right music and the right beverages, even the worst hangovers are quickly forgotten and the laughing and fun begins among friends. These days, brunch often start as early as 10:30 or 11:00 and has been known to continue late into the afternoon or even early evening. If you have a somewhat stocked pantry, you can easily throw together the perfect brunch gathering followed by the afternoon grill-out or just lounge by the pool and enjoy people and the many stories that come forth. I guarantee with good food and drink, there will be lots of laughing and more unforgettable memories.

Brunch allows you to combine your absolute favorites from both breakfast and lunch and create that oh just so perfect meal. There is nothing better than being able to have eggs and bacon, followed by salami slices and cheese followed by pork loin and then finishing it all up with some amazing strawberry gelatin salad and a piece of carrot cake!

The best part about having people over for brunch or preparing brunch for folks is that there are very few 'rules' about brunch other than good food, good conversation and most importantly good fun. You should always consider brunch your chance to experiment as well as to try new things. Brunch allows you to dare to be different. After all, some of those folks are hung over and are just glad someone else is doing the cooking. Hung over or not, the one consistent thing about brunches is that once people

get a taste for a good brunch, they will want you to invite them again and again and again. For me, the only way I can respond to that is to say, "Why not?!!"

Setting up for brunch can be just as fun as preparing it. Get creative with a whole heap of different items to create a centerpiece or get fun and fabulous with placemats, place cards, napkins or any other table linens. People always appreciate the time and effort you put into making a meal a bit more special. So, go ahead and make it all a Whole Heap more special and let those around you know how much you care.

Beignets

A quick and easy basic breakfast to start with. These delicious morsels are easy to prepare and are easier to eat.

1 and 1/3 cups flour
1 teaspoon baking powder
1 egg
Salt to taste
Water for desired consistency

Consistency of your batter should be similar to that of pancake batter. Mix ingredients. Drop spoonfuls at a time into hot grease and fry till golden brown. Plate and sprinkle powdered sugar on top.

Healthy Bran Muffins

Our family has called these lil' morsels so many different things. Mom has called them fiber bombs, Kevin has called them banana muffins and I call them breakfast or a healthy snack. Mom got the recipe from a friend. These are moist, delicious and when they are hot out of the oven, holy smoke, I can eat 6 of them. These are the perfect muffins for a brunch. If you make them the evening before, they will store easily and be just as moist and delicious the next day when you pop over to a friend or family member's home for brunch. Being much healthier than most muffins I like making, they pair perfectly with hot coffee or ice cold milk.

2 cups All Bran® cereal
3/4 cup skim milk
1 cup chunky applesauce
2 mashed bananas
1/2 cup Splenda®
1/2 cup loose brown sugar
1/2 cup whole wheat flour
1/2 cup self-rising flour
1 teaspoon baking soda
1 teaspoon cinnamon
1/2 teaspoon baking powder

Put milk in microwave until just warm. Add milk to All Bran. Let sit 5 minutes. Add remaining ingredients. Bake at 325° for 40-45 minutes. Told ya it was easy.

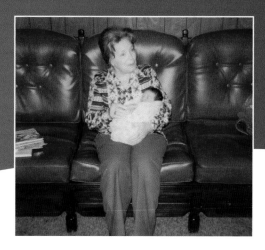

Grandma's Cornbread Waffles

With no offense here, Grandma was not a great cook. Grandma was dad's mom and she was an awesome woman. I remember her as fiercely independent, stylish, and unwaveringly Catholic. Her home and her garden were always perfect and anyone from the neighborhood was welcome to visit. I even got my first car from her. But a great cook, never. She loved College Inn, one of my old favorites in New Orleans. Grandma also LOVED her cornbread waffles AND so did I. These were warm, fluffy and OH SO GOOD. The finishing touch was heating up Steen's cane syrup and pouring it over the butter covered waffles. How could any of this be wrong?

1 ½ cups yellow corn meal
4 teaspoons baking powder
2 tablespoons sugar
1 ½ cups milk
3 tablespoons melted butter

¾ cup of white flour
½ teaspoon salt
½ teaspoon baking soda
2 eggs

Mix all dry ingredients, Beat eggs and milk together and stir gently into dry mixture. Add melted butter and pour 5 to 6 tablespoons at a time into preheated waffle iron. Cook for 3 min and(YUM) enjoy

Hint: There are so many ways to make these even more fabulous than they currently are. I have used everything from canned fig preserves to strawberries, bananas, blueberries, and even canned pears, to top these off. The cornbread goes well with everything and allows me to eat according to whatever mood I may be in at whatever time I am eating. I have even topped these with crumbled bacon and blue cheese for a savory dinner flavor.

Kevin's Killer Hash Brown Egg Bake

My brother started this one! He was never a great cook but every now and then he blows me away. There are a few of his Big Braller recipes in here and this is one of them! I have got to say Kevin is one of the most fearless people I know in a kitchen. He will try ANYTHING when it comes to food. He will try anything, mix whatever flavors or whatever ingredients he has at hand to make anything he can. Now when he or I visit home we are sure to wake up one morning with the

smell of one of the family egg bakes in the oven. What a way to start a day!

1 - 32 ounce package of frozen hash brown cubes
1 - cup of extra sharp cheddar cheese shredded – If you love cheese like me add another ½ cup
1 - pound of cooked crumbled BACON – or add a bit more because everything is better with bacon!!!
1 - small red bell pepper chopped
1 - small green bell pepper chopped
½ - cup chopped green onions
¼ - cup chopped parsley
¾ - teaspoon salt
¾ - teaspoon ground black pepper
8 - eggs
2 - cups of milk
1 - teaspoon Louisiana hot sauce
½ - teaspoon paprika

Preheat oven to 350 degrees. In a large bowl mix hash browns, bacon, ½ of the cheese, peppers, green onions, parsley, salt, pepper and hot sauce. Pour this mixture into a 13 x 9 x 2 baking dish. Now mix eggs and milk in another bowl and beat well. Pour the egg and milk mixture over the hash brown mixture and bake for 45 to 50 minutes – until top begins to turn golden brown. Remove from oven and cover with remaining half of cheese and throw in oven for 3 minutes more. Remove cut and serve!!!

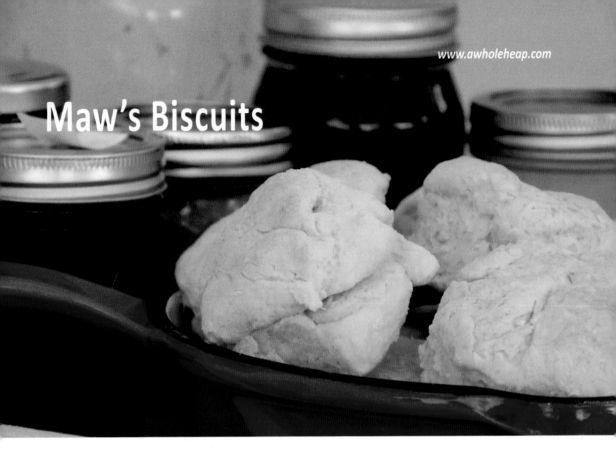

Maw's Biscuits

Now here is a story for ya'll. My brother and I grew up in Metarie, an extension of New Orleans. The rest of our extended family lived just outside of a small town in Southwest Louisiana called Rayne (yes, actually outside of the small town and not in it). About once a month, mom and dad would throw us into the back of the Station Wagon on a Friday evening and we would go and spend the weekend with Maw and Paw and all of our aunts, uncles, and cousins. We would make the drive to Rayne in just under 2 and a half hours. Because of the small house that maw and paw lived in – the very one my mother grew up in – Kevin and I slept on the pull-out sofa or on the floor of the living room right next to Paw's recliner and just outside of maw's kitchen. Without failure, by 6 am every Saturday morning maw was in the kitchen. She would open the squeaky door of the oven, drag the large cast iron skillet across the rack and WHAM, slam it down on the countertop. I was now awake for the day.

Of course, I would walk into the kitchen in utter amazement to watch the rituals that Maw would go through. The coffee was already on, and Paw had already made it out of the front door and into the garden. Maw would smile and say "come give me a lil t-beck," a little kiss on the cheek for those of you who do not know what this is. By this time she already had 2 thin Corelle® coffee cups out. I would give her a hug and a peck on the cheek and she would ask me if I wanted a little coffee. Wanting to be grown up, I always said yes and she would pour about a quarter of the cup up with coffee, heat some milk and fill the rest of the cup with the steamy milk and about 4 coffee spoons of sugar. The next logical part of the ritual was of course my asking of the question: "Maw, are you gonna make us some biscuits?" She would always smile and I knew the best was yet to come. The ritual began with the handfuls of flour hitting the counter and always ended with me happily cutting out biscuits with a juice glass. I lost maw on July 1 199X.... I have 2 treasured possessions from her. One is drawing of her biscuit recipe that she gave me one year for my birthday and the other is one of the very skillets that used to wake me up when it hit the countertop on those amazing Saturday mornings.

4 cups of flour
2/3 cup solid Crisco®
1 teaspoon salt
2 tablespoons sugar
2 tablespoons baking powder
1 cup of milk

Stir dry ingredients and Crisco together BY HAND until mixed thoroughly. For this process I often use a wooden spoon that I have coated in vegetable oil so it does not absorb the oil in the ingredients. Then add milk and GENTLY stir.

On a floured surface – I always use my baking cutting board – flatten out with your hands until biscuits are about ¾ of an inch to one inch thick– I use my hands to do this because It was not too often that I saw Maw Maw use a rolling pin... Place on an ungreased pan and bake at 400 for 20 to 25 minutes

Maw always used a small water glass to cut her biscuits out and cooked them in a cast iron skillet, which I now have and will always treasure. Cut your biscuits out and place them in a seasoned cast iron skillet and bake for 15 to 20 minutes in an oven set to 350 degrees.

Once you remove these from the oven, be ready with your butter and even more importantly be ready with fig preserves or your favorite jar of preserves in order to fully enjoy these right out of the oven. It makes me hungry just writing about them.

Happy Birthday

FLOUR.

SKILETTE.

MILK

BACKIN POWER.

CRISCO.

BOIL.

ROLLIA PIN.

I am sorry I couldint get to town
to buy you a card. so I made you
one to keep for a saucener of me
so it will remind you when I
made my Biskut
Love mo. I love you very
much. ha ha.

Fun Fruit Salad

Several years ago on a trip home to visit mom and Jeff I got to try this yummy dish. This delicious salad has amazing flavor and I have put it on biscuits, waffles, pancakes or yogurt. I have also served it as a dessert after an amazing meal. I promise you this is one to really enjoy and most importantly share! I always find this to be a wonderfully fun and colorful dish to bring to a friend's house for brunch! This also holds up well in the refrigerator and can be enjoyed all week. Many times I double the recipe and keep half at home and bring half to brunch. It is part breakfast and part dessert – So you decide.

1 10 ounce box of frozen sliced strawberries in light syrup – thawed
1 20 ounce can of pineapple chunks in juice drained
1 11 ounce can mandarin orange slices drained
1 21 ounce can peach pie filling
3 bananas peeled and sliced into rounds

Pour strawberries and syrup into large bowl. Add the pineapple chunks and the orange slices and stir in the pie filling. Chill in the refrigerator for 4 hours or overnight and then stir in sliced bananas before serving. This dish adds plenty of color and flavor to the table so be sure to serve in a large glass dish so your friends and family can see this fantastic dish!

Mom's French Toast

Another childhood memory that I think of and smile is mom making French toast. Mom worked and had to leave by 730, yet she still made time to make Kevin and I breakfast every morning. This French toast was never anything special from a recipe point of view. Its special in that that took the time and put her love into something so simple and yet something that I love to eat even to this day. Mom even took the time There are many ways to prepare this basic yummy breakfast treat and it is one that I often enjoy making when I have friends visiting from out of town. A change from the way I had this delicious breakfast growing up is that now I don't have Bunny Bread available but I do have a few AMAZING bakeries close by. I often use a fresh baked loaf of bread and find myself using a variety of different kinds. I use cinnamon raisin, a good sourdough and my most recent discovery for French Toast is using a cranberry walnut bread.

2 eggs (for richer toast you may use 3 eggs)
1 ½ cups whole milk
1 teaspoon cinnamon
1 tablespoon melted butter
¼ teaspoon vanilla extract

Mix all ingredients in a bowl and set aside. Slice your bread about an inch think. Place bread in bowl and let sit for a few seconds in order to soak everything up. Flip bread over. Melt some butter in a pan over medium heat and drop toast in pan and let cook for about 3 minutes. Flip over and cook for another 3 minutes. Repeat for 1 minute or until golden brown. Remove French toast from pan and sprinkle with cinnamon and sugar! Now make as much as you need and feast away! I know you will love this one and always remember you can add bananas warmed in butter over the top, or fresh berries, warm cane syrup or whatever you like to make this delicious dish even better!!

Maw Maw's Cornbread

This is yet another one of my favorites from Maw. I always use one of my prized possessions, a well-seasoned cast iron skillet, for this one. There is nothing better to warm the body and soul than a piece of cornbread, fresh out of the oven. I remember watching the bitter melt across the cornbread once it was sliced open. On particularly cold days, I remember hot cornbread mixed into a bowl of hot milk to make a delicious belly-warming treat. It never ceases to amaze me how nostalgic Mom gets every time she talks about Maw's cornbread. I immediately get story after story about her memories of cornbread. I often flash back to dad's face lighting up with a hot piece of cornbread that he would slice open and pour on some amazing Steen's Cane syrup! I use this cornbread for my cornbread dressing and any other recipe that would call for yummy cornbread.

1 ½ cups of yellow corn meal
1 ½ cups flour
5 teaspoons of baking powder
1 ½ teaspoons salt
1 ½ cup milk
2 capfuls of white vinegar
3 eggs
1/3 cup of oil

Pour 2 capfuls of vinegar in the milk and stir well. This process makes your buttermilk.

Mix all ingredients. Pour about 3 teaspoons of oil in the bottom of your skillet and heat for 2 minutes in the oven. Pour in batter and bake at 350 for about 15 minutes or until golden brown. Remove and be ready with butter and even more importantly, some good old fashioned cane syrup!

Monkey Bread

Another favorite of mine from our many visits to Rayne was this delicious sweet fun food. Mom's sister, Aunt Bea, would often make this sweet treat that works for breakfast, snack, lunch, snack, dinner, snack, or even a late night snack...Hahahaha. I would often sneak this treat right off of the counter at Maw's. I LOVE this sweet treat because of the many shapes and ways you can create. I have even done a double recipe and stacked them on top of each other. The sweet sugar fantastic cinnamon and buttery taste just makes this great with coffee or tea first thing in the morning!

3 10 packs of biscuits in a can
½ cup melted butter
1 cup sugar
½ cup brown sugar
2 teaspoons cinnamon
1 cup f chopped pecans

Generously Grease a tube pan and preheat oven to 350°. Place melted butter in a shallow bowl and mix all sugars and cinnamon and pour onto a dinner plate.

Roll biscuits into balls about the size of a golf ball. Dip dough balls into melted butter and roll in sugar mixture. Arrange 4 or 5 at a time spacing about a ½ inch apart in the pan. Repeat, and make into layers sprinkling nuts between the layers. When done sprinkle the remaining sugar mixture over the top.

Bake at 350° for 45 min to an hour....If you notice top getting too brown cover with foil. Remove from oven when done and IMMEDIATELY remove from tube pan. YUMMY!

Layered Fruit Salad

Sounds healthy right? Well it's fruit, of course it's healthy. It's just everything else you mix with it that can make it not so healthy. I have often brought this dish out to brunches because it is fun and eye catching. I often find myself experimenting with the variations of fruit and fillings to make the dish more seasonal. Many people often ask why I bake this dish. Believe it or not, it makes it easier to present, especially if you fruit that can "turn ugly on you," like bananas or apples., Baking the dish browns it all not to mention the process really mixes all of the flavors through the layers of the "salad." This is one of those recipes that is SO much fun to experiment with as you can create these from A to Z and 99.9% of the time it will taste absolutely delicious.

2 red apple – I tend to use Fuji or Blackburns
2 green apple – Granny Smith
2 or 3 bananas
1 mango
½ cup brown sugar
1/3 cup honey
½ cup rolled quick oats
2 tablespoon butter

Slice all fruit. Spread 1 tablespoon butter on bottom of round casserole dish. Place sliced mangos on the bottom then ¼ cup dried oats. Layer in apples then sprinkle brown sugar over. Finally place banana slices over the top, drizzle honey over the top and sprinkle remainder of oats on top.
Bake at 350° for 45 minutes and enjoy!

Strawberry Delight

2 6 ounce strawberry Jell-O®
2 cups boiling water
2 10 ounce packages of frozen sliced strawberries thawed
1 4 ounce can of crushed pineapple
3 medium bananas mashed
1 coarsely chopped nuts – I use pecans or walnuts
12 ounces cream cheese
1 ¼ cups of sour cream

In a large bowl stir gelatin and boiling water together, add the strawberries with the juice. Drain the pineapple and add along with bananas and nuts. Pour half of this mixture into a 12x8x2 dish and refrigerate until firm. Soften cream cheese and combine it with the sour cream and spread it evenly over the first layer. Gently spoon remaining mixture over the creamed mixture. Chill again until firm. Serve on lettuce leaf or as a dessert.

Mom's Awesome Hot Pepper Jelly

3 large green bell peppers cubed
3 cayenne peppers green or red
1 ½ cups cider vinegar
6 ½ cups of sugar
1 bottle liquid pectin
Green or red food coloring

Remove seeds from all peppers. Put vinegar and peppers in blender and blend away! Pour into sauce pan and add sugar. Bring to a rolling boil for 3 minutes stirring occasionally. Remove from heat and let cool for 2 minutes. Remove any foam on top of mixture. Add pectin and food coloring of your choice until mixture has your desired color. Stir for 2 more minutes. Pour into HOT sterilized jelly jars and seal. This will make 6, 8 ounce jars.

I have always been a fan of sweet and spicy foods. When mom took this delicious treat out of the pantry on a Sunday, it meant we were having company and I would get one of my favorite little appetizers. Mom let a block of cream cheese come to room temperature then spoon the pepper jelly over the cream cheese and serve it with wheat crackers. i still get excited when I see all those jellies in her pantry. I hope you enjoy them the way I do!

Hint: I always make a batch of red and a batch of green. These are amazing host/hostess gifts for dinner guests during the holidays!

Russian Spice Tea

Ok here is a quick and easy way to get your kids to drink something wonderful on a cold day. I have to be honest here, I still get excited every Christmas because I know that in my stocking – yes I still get Christmas stocking – will be a jar of this most wonderful, soul-warming, elixir. As corny as this whole thing sounds, this easy powered mixture is a sure-fire way to create memories of warmth on a cold winter's day. Now living in sunny south Florida, I look forward to an evening where the temperature gets below 60 so I can break out my jar, start up a kettle of water and spoon in two orange mounds of spicy goodness.

This concoction makes a wonderful host or hostess gift throughout the holidays. A simple jarful with ribbon can spread the warmth. . I love this with Dad's favorite fruit cookies, Maw's biscuits, Old fashioned tea cakes, mom's French toast and so many more. The sugar can be left out completely if you like and you can add it to your tea once it is hot.

18 ounce container of Tang®
¾ cup of instant tea
1 package of lemonade mix... I usually use Kool-Aid®
1 cup of sugar
2 teaspoons cinnamon
½ teaspoon ground cloves

Mix and store...when you are ready boil water and add to your favorite mug and add 2 teaspoons of dry mix and enjoy. If you crave sugar, add a teaspoon!

Hot Beverages

Hot Spice Tea

7 small tea bags
4 sticks of cinnamon
1 tablespoon whole cloves
Steep tea for 20 minutes and pour into a gallon container

Add 1 small can frozen orange juice
1 small can frozen lemonade
2 cups pineapple juice
2 cups sugar

Fill the remaining space of the gallon with water. Refrigerate and heat as needed in the microwave.

Hot Citrus Tea

2 cups of water
1 ½ quart
½ cup lemon juice
1 ½ cups sugar

6 whole cloves
8 tea bags
2/3 cup orange juice

Combine 2 cups water and cloves in a sauce pan and bring to a boil, remove from heat and let stand for 2 hours. Bring 1 ½ quart of water to a boil in large sauce pan, add tea bags remove from heat and over let stand for 5 to 10 minutes remove tea bags.

Strain clove mixture and add tea stir in juice and sugar and let stand for 1 hour before using.

Brunch Punch

Champagne Punch

- 1 bottle of Champagne
- 16 ounces of orange juice
- 8 ounces pineapple juice
- 12 ounces (1 can) ginger ale or sprite
- 8 ounces of sliced strawberries

Make sure all ingredients are very cold. Pour together and serve with strawberry slice. To make the punch a tad more colorful, I have been known to drop in other fresh fruit pieces such as pineapple or even a couple of fresh peach slices. No matter what you do, people will love it. Let's be real now, there's champagne in it!

Fruit Punch

- 1 bottle of Champagne OR 16 ounces of rum
- 2 cups of sugar
- 1 48 ounce can of orange juice
- 1 48 ounce can pineapple juice
- 4 to 6 bananas
- 2 teaspoons lemon juice

Make simple syrup with water and sugar. Add juices and mix in mashed bananas well, then add to liquid, now add lemon juice. Freeze in appropriate containers and then place in bowl and pour ginger ale over top and enjoy.

Chill in the refrigerator for 4 hours or overnight and then stir in sliced bananas before serving. This punch adds plenty of color and flavor to the table so be sure to serve in a large glass dish so your friends and family can see this fantastic creation!

APPETIZERS

Artichoke Dip

This dip is one of a few recipes that are in this book from one of my mom's very dear friends, Diane. We lost her recently and every time I prepare one of these recipes or look outside at my white bird of paradise plant from her, I think of a wonderful and dear friend who we all miss. This rich and creamy dip is super easy and even more delicious. I always switch my serving of this dish using roasted toast points, water crackers or wheat crackers. Yes I have even served this hot bubbly dip with celery. If you can spoon it onto it you can serve it with this creamy richness.

1 8 ounce cream cheese
1 ½ cans artichoke hearts drained and dried
2 tablespoons butter
3 cloves garlic chopped
3 green onions chopped
½ cup shredded Parmesan cheese

Sauté artichokes in butter for 5 minutes on medium heat and then set aside. Spread cream cheese on 9 inch glass pie dish. Place green onion and garlic on top of cream cheese. Place artichokes on top of onions and garlic. Sprinkle cheese on top, place in microwave and cook on full power for 4 ½ to 5 ½ minutes. Be very careful when removing this dish from the microwave because the dish will be HOT HOT HOT!!!

Artichoke Balls

A fantastic finger food for parties this can easily be prepared ahead of time and enjoyed the whole evening through. This appetizer is a must-have when throwing parties. I almost always double this recipe as these tend to be a hit with guests.

- 2 cans of artichoke hearts drained and mashed
- 2 large eggs lightly beaten
- 2 tablespoons of olive oil
- 3 or 4 cloves of garlic
- 1 cup Italian bread crumbs
- 1 cup of Romaine or Parmesan cheese

On medium heat I sauté oil and for about 3 minutes, and add artichoke hearts. Add eggs and stir constantly for 5 minutes or eggs will scramble. Turn off heat and add ½ cup bread crumbs and ½ cup of the cheese. Form into small balls. Pour other ½ cup of bread crumbs and ½ cup of cheese into clean shallow bowl and roll formed balls into mixture.

Hints – Depending on the crowd you can also add one ten ounce package of thawed and well drained chopped spinach to this recipe and create artichoke and spinach balls. Or add sautéed onions, peppers, or some Lousiana Hot Sauce for spice. See there are so many ways to make food Wholly Yours!

I ALWAYS make these 2 or 3 days ahead of time and store in the refrigerator. The evening of the party remove from the refrigerator and place on serving dish and let come to room temperature (usually about an hour). Watch your guests go nuts!

Bacon Cheese Wraps

I was teaching summer school in Dallas years ago and went to a family's home for dinner one Sunday. These delicious morsels were served and I just had to know how to make them. Crisp bacon, toasty bread, and warm smooth goodness on the inside... the simple yet perfect combination made this a wonderful bite that I have made over and over again. This is one that I highly recommend you play with. If there is a flavor you like or want to try, this is a fast inexpensive way to test your desire to try something new and different. Make it Wholly Yours! Some would say this is a childish recipe but let's face it... It has bacon and I LOVE me some bacon!

1 8 ounce cream cheese
1 pack of green onions
1 tablespoon chopped garlic
2 teaspoons balsamic glaze
1 pound of your favorite bacon
1 loaf of white sandwich bread

Mix first 4 ingredients well until light and fluffy. Cut crusts off of bread and then spread cream cheese mixture on 1 side of each slice of bread. Roll each piece and then wrap with 1 slice of bacon. Bake on 350° until bacon is crispy. Usually about 12 to 15 minutes. Arrange these on a tray and watch your guests fight over this ridciulously delightful treat. I mean come one, who doesn't like Bacon.

New Orleans Most Famous Sandwich- My Mini Muffuletta

There are always foods that can take me home in a heartbeat and the muffuletta is one of them. I often make a pig of myself with these fantastic sandwiches. This uniquely New Orleans sandwich is often a staple at cocktail parties, receptions, holiday parties and just about any other time or place that a bunch of New Orleanians get together. Most recently was the wedding of one of my best friends. Johnny and Stacey's wedding reception was beautiful and simply perfect in every way. For me one of the many touches that made it so were the deliciously warm just so perfect mini muffulettas. So put these finger sized minis together, put some good music on, invite some friends and look out because you are sure to pass a good time with these New Orleans favorites.

2 dozen small dinner rolls preferably with sesame seeds
A 32 ounce jar of olive salad
12 slices of Swiss cheese cut in half
12 slices of provolone cheese cut in half
24 slices of Genoa salami
24 slices deli ham

Cut rolls in half and place bottoms on large pan and place 1 heaping spoonful of olive salad on each followed by one of the halved slices of Swiss cheese. Next, place 1 slice of each meat on top of Swiss. Finally top with provolone cheese and cover with bun tops.

Hints – Since I LOVE Garlic I often place 1 VERY thin slice of garlic on top before the last slice of cheese. I have also known people to place a bit of crumbled cooked bacon on these before putting bun tops on. Finally you can place a toothpick through a small olive on the top.

Serving Hint – I OFTEN cook these the day before serving and seal them in zip top bags in the refrigerator and keep the bun tops out of the refrigerator in a zip top bag until I'm ready to serve them. Remove from refrigerator and let come to room temperature OR place in oven on 200° and heat the Bottoms ONLY for 10 to 12 minutes to warm them a bit and slightly melt the cheese. YUM

Marinated Checkerboard Cheese

This is a SUPER simple recipe. Guests tend to LOVE this one! Whether you are hosting people or heading out to someone else's place, this is an easy thing to do that people enjoy, not to mention they think you took forever to prepare it. Garnish with fresh herbs and place on a fabulous plate. Make this at least the night before you will serve. This is a sure winner for both you and your guests.

½ cup very good olive oil – I LOVE a good Greek olive oil
¼ cup white wine vinegar
1 2 ounce jar pimentos
3 tablespoons green onions chopped fine
3 tablespoons fresh parsley chopped fine
4 toes of garlic chopped fine
1 teaspoon sugar
½ teaspoon salt
½ teaspoon freshly ground pepper
¾ teaspoon basil chopped fine

Mix all above ingredients well with a wire whisk and set aside.

1 8 ounce cream cheese
1 8 ounce block sharp or extra sharp cheddar cheese

Cut blocks of cheese in half lengthwise. Then cut cheeses into equal sized blocks. I usually get about 6 to 8 across each block. Arrange cheese cubes onto serving plate alternating cheeses. Whisk mixture again and pour over the top of the cheese. Place dish in refrigerator overnight and serve the following day!

Crab Dip

- ½ stick of butter melted
- ¼ cup finely chopped white onion
- ¼ cup finely chopped celery
- 3 cloves garlic pressed
- 2 tablespoons finely chopped parsley
- 1 tablespoon Worcestershire® sauce
- ½ teaspoon salt
- ½ teaspoon Louisiana Hot Sauce
- 1 8 ounce cream cheese
- 1 pound white lump crabmeat

Sauté onion, celery and garlic in butter until soft and clear. Add parsley, Worcestershire, salt and hot sauce and now melt in cream cheese. Fold in 1 pound of white lump crabmeat and mix for 3 more minutes on medium heat.

Hot and Fast Crab Dip

This is one of those recipes that I whip up as soon as someone suggests that 'maybe we should do dinner tonight'. This is a failsafe, fast and easy recipe that every beginner can do and feel proud of what they made.

- 2 tablespoons melted butter
- 1 8 ounce cream cheese softened
- 1 cup shredded Swiss cheese
- ½ cup mayonnaise
- ½ pound drained crabmeat
- 2 green onions chopped
- 2 cloves of garlic finely chopped
- 2 teaspoons Louisiana Hot Sauce

Mix all together until well blended. Coat bottom of a pie plate or oven safe dish with the melted butter. Pour in crab mixture and spread out. Bake in oven on 350° for 15 minutes. Stir mixture about half way through. Remove from oven for 3 minutes and turn on broiler and broil until LIGHTLY browned – about 2 minutes. BE VERY CAREFUL when removing this is one HOT dish after the broiler!!!

Pecan Cranberry Spread

1 cup cream cheese softened
1/2 cup chopped pecans
1/2 cup dried cranberries
1/4 cup of orange juice concentrate

Using electric mixer, beat at medium speed until cheeses is soft and fluffy. Put in a bowl and add remaining ingredients and stir. Cover and refrigerate for 30 minutes. Makes 2 cups.

FAST and Friendly Dip

Now this one comes from a dear friend of Jeff's straight out of the Midwest in Blair, Nebraska. This is fast easy recipe that I use for unexpected guests.

3 cans of whole sweet kernel corn drained
3 blocks of cream cheese softened
8 green onions chopped
1 Small can of sliced black olives drained
2 teaspoons crushed red pepper
2 teaspoons chopped garlic

Throw in a large bowl, mix well and serve. This is also GREAT if refrigerated for 2 or more hours!

Chutneys, Pesto and Salsa O My!

OK the following recipes are some of the most versatile out there.
It never ceases to amaze me how I fall back on these tried and true favorites. Whether
I am having two or twenty over to the house, I have a tendency to prepare one of the
following recipes. Chutneys and salsas are perfect dishes to prepare to work on your knife
skills as well. I use chutney, pesto and salsa for a variety of purposes. They are perfect
companions to toasted breads, on crackers, tortilla or pita chips. For main courses they
can mix well with pasta, be used to dress, fish, chicken or pork. Many can be served warm,
cold or room temperature, it's all about choices. I also LOVE to experiment here. These
are a bit more labor intensive
to make BUT they are often
very inexpensive to experiment
with flavor. The following
recipes are sure fire wins, BUT I
encourage you to try your own
combinations and or spins on
them or create your own and
let me know how it goes!
I often get asked to help
people who want to learn how
to cook. I find the following
recipes great fun to teach as
the fantastically fresh flavors
in these recipes will make you
want to prepare them and
experiment over and over and
over again.

Cantaloupe Chutney

1/2 large cantaloupe peeled, seeded and diced (about 4 cups)
1 shallot diced
1/2 cup firmly packed light brown sugar
1/4 cup white wine vinegar
1 tablespoon minced fresh ginger or 1/4 teaspoon of ground ginger
2 garlic cloves mined
1/4 teaspoon salt
1/4 teaspoon ground red pepper
2 tablespoons chopped fresh mint

Combine first 8 ingredients in a large non-aluminum saucepan. Bring to a boil. Reduce heat and cook uncovered over medium-low heat 50 minutes or until thickened, stirring often. Cool slightly; stir in mint. Cover and chill at least 2 hours.

Cilantro Pesto

1/2 cup chopped pecans
2 cups loosely packed fresh cilantro leaves
1/3 cup olive oil
2 garlic cloves
1/2 teaspoon salt

1 teaspoon cumin seeds
1/2 cup grated Parmesan cheese
1/4 cup cold water
1 tablespoon lemon juice

Bake pecans in a single layer in a shallow pan for 5 to 6 minutes at 350 degrees or until toasted and fragrant, stirring halfway through. Cool 10 minutes. Meanwhile, place a small skillet over medium-high heat until hot; add cumin seeds and cook, stirring constantly 1 to 2 minutes or until toasted. Cool 10 minutes.

Process pecans, cumin seeds and next 7 ingredients in a food processor until smooth, stopping to scrape down sides as needed.

Olive Pesto

1 (7 ounce) jar pitted Kalamata olives, drained
1 (7 ounce) jar pimento stuffed Spanish olives, drained
1/4 cup grated Parmesan cheese
3 tablespoons olive oil
2 tablespoons Balsamic vinegar
3 to 4 garlic cloves
1 teaspoon pepper
1 teaspoon smoked paprika

Process all ingredients in a food processor until smooth, stopping to scrape down sides as needed.

Your Own Ideas

Sun Dried Tomato Pesto

2 (3 ounce) packages of sun dried tomato halves
1/2 cup grated Parmesan cheese
1/2 cup loosely packed fresh flat leaf parsley
1/2 cup olive oil
1/4 cup pine nuts
3 garlic cloves
3 tablespoons cold water
1 tablespoon lemon juice

Process all ingredients in a food processor until smooth, stopping to scrape down sides as needed.

Now for the kicker, use your pesto creations on pasta, toast points or even spread over your favorite cheese for a whole new heap of a twist! The more creative you get with pesto the better. You simply need to blend some of your favorite flavors and blend away and make your magic happen.

Fresh Mango Salsa

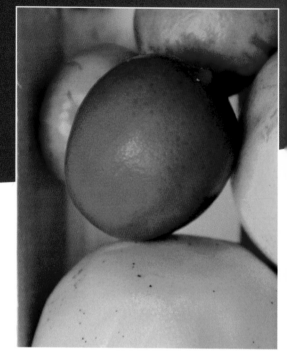

2 ripe mangoes cubed
1/2 red bell pepper, finely chopped
1/2 small red onion, finely chopped
3 tablespoons chopped fresh parsley
2 to 3 tablespoons of chopped fresh mint
1 jalapeno pepper seeded and minced
2 tablespoons of fresh lime juice
1/2 teaspoon salt
1/4 teaspoon pepper

Stir together all ingredients. Cover and chill 3 hours. Makes 2 1/2 cups.
Substitute 1 (26 ounce) jar mango slices drained or pineapple if desired.

Corn Salsa

4 medium ears, fresh corn, husks removed
1 12 ounce jar roasted red peppers, drained and chopped
2 green onions, finely chopped
1 large tomato, seeded and minced
1 jalapeno pepper, seeded and minced
3 tablespoons minced fresh parsley
2 tablespoons fresh lime juice
1 tablespoon white wine vinegar
1/2 teaspoon salt
1/4 teaspoon pepper
1/4 teaspoon ground cumin

Cut corn from cobs. Combine corn and remaining ingredients in a large bowl.
Cover and chill at least 2 hours. Makes 4 cups.

Mild to Medium Salsa

4 peeled tomatoes
1 large onion
3 yellow chilies
1 small can mild chopped green mild chilies
2 or 3 cloves of garlic chopped well
1 tablespoon sugar
4 teaspoons salt
3 tablespoons olive oil
3 tablespoons vinegar

Chop all and mix well. Do not blend in blender. This will be a fairly mild salsa. Always feel free to add the heat as you see fit. I often add 1 or two chopped chipotle chilies to the mixture. Twist – Grill your tomatoes and onion and yellow peppers for a little extra zing of flavor!

Sausage Balls

Another recipe that is perfect for an appetizer and is actually something you can keep a bag of in your freezer and take out when you have company coming by. Also a family favorite, sausage balls were started by my Aunt Bea. Her youngest son Mitch and I can make ourselves sick sitting there eating these until they are gone! It would not be the holidays if sausage balls were not a part of the many many things we serve. I have seen these in a variety of settings with a few different twists using a multitude of cheeses as well as different meats. These are the perfect little finger food since they are bite sized and not messy at all. I try and make these as often as possible as I love them and thus far, I have not had a gathering where they have not been the singular hit of the evening. I bet so many of you will pull this recipe out when you host your next get together and I just know you will enjoy them.

1 pound sharp cheddar cheese
1 pound hot pork sausage
2 ½ cups Bisquick® mix

Grate cheese, break sausage up into small pieces mix into Bisquick® mix with hands. I knead the living heck out of this mixture in one of my stainless steel bowls and find the more you knead it the easier it is to make the balls. Roll into small bite sized balls. Always remember that these will grow a bit in the oven so be sure and not make these too big as you want your guests to be able to pop them into their mouths.

Bake at 375° for 15 to 20 minutes or until they start to brown.

Hint: I always make these a day or two before the party and keep them tightly covered in the refrigerator and take them out 1 hour before cooking to get them close to room temperature. For a touch of added drama, shocker I know, grate some fresh parmesan cheese over the tops of these on your serving dish.

Nanny's Sausage Bread

Now this is one for the books. I have had many nicknames growing up but one of those nicknames was from Nanny (my Aunt Net). She used to call me Jaws. She knew that when I liked something there was nothing that would stop me from eating and eating and eating. This was one of those things that I simply couldn't get enough of. This is a recipe that makes me think of my Nanny (godmother) every time. . It has three of my favorite things; bread, meat and cheese! The first time I had this treat, I was in heaven. This amazing appetizer is filling enough to be served as a lunch. Every one of my cousins LOVES this dish. Every time nanny make this everyone is hoping to stops by and grab a few slices. I have never known her to be able to make less than 2 whole loaves,

and there is never a single piece left over. Even more fantastic now are the memories of making this with my mom. This is a bit of work but I promise the reward is most certainly there.

YES I CHEAT! I use store bought bread dough all of the time on this one. I have never professed to be some sort of incredible bread maker so I cheat with the dough but believe you me, this stuff is a hit. I have done this recipe a few dozen different ways but here is the original one that helped me to fall in love with it . I dare you. Bring this to a friend's house for a football game or a poker night. Everyone will love it; unless they are vegetarians.

Nanny's Sausage Bread

1 pound roll of sausage
1 pound salami chopped
1 pound ham chopped
1 small can of sliced black olives
Small can or jar pimentos
1 small 4 ounce can Jalapeno peppers rinsed and chopped
Garlic powder
12 ounces mozzarella cheese grated
12 ounces cheddar cheese grated
3 loaves frozen bread dough

Thaw loaves and let rise. Brush the dough with melted butter. Roll loaves out to about ¼ inch thick and brush with butter again. Fill with ingredients being sure to leave about 2 inches to seal the roll. Fold over and pinch, brush again with butter and cook until top crust is golden brown, usually about 40 minutes at 350 degrees.

Shrimp Appetizers

The next few recipes are always yummy. I have always loved shrimp. No matter how you cook them I will eat them. I have eaten them raw to fried and everywhere in between (my mom will laugh at that line!). I can remember many a day when growing up where mom would get a phone call that a friend's husband or neighbor had just arrived home and had ice chests full of good ole Gulf of Mexico shrimp ready to go. Mom would grab her purse and ask if I wanted to go and out the door we would go.

I have got to admit that we were spoiled with the availability of fresh Gulf shrimp. Mom would often de-head and devein the shrimp and freeze them in zip lock filled with water. The best part of watching this ritual was that I knew we were going to have these prepared one way or another that very evening. The one thing I often have an issue with is that every store under the sun now sells these cooked shrimp platters. Let's remember all they do is boil or steam the shrimp and there is little to NO flavor on them.

Here you are given the perfect gift of an opportunity for exploration. Pull that spice rack out or head out into your yard or garden and go after those herbs that you love so much and use them with those shrimp. Create something special for those you care about. Trust me when they notice the fresh flavors, they will ask how you did it ,and, when you tell them, they will feel special.

Lemon-herbed Pickled Shrimp

2 tablespoons whole grain mustard
1/2 cup tarragon vinegar
1/4 cup chopped fresh dill
1/4 cup chopped fresh tarragon
1/2 teaspoon salt
1/2 teaspoon ground black pepper
2 pounds large fresh shrimp cooked and peeled, tails left on
3 lemons divided

In a large glass bowl, whisk together mustard and vinegar. Add dill, tarragon, salt and pepper; whisking well. Add shrimp, tossing gently to coat. Zest and juice 1 lemon. Add lemon zest and juice to shrimp mixture, tossing gently to combine.

Slice remaining lemons.

Add to shrimp mixture, stirring gently to combine. Cover and refrigerate for at least 8 hours and up to 48 hours.

Shrimp Fritters

I have the best time serving this when I have a fellow southerner or two around. These are little drops of fried heaven! I often prepare this dish outdoors so as not to have a grease smell in the house when my guests arrive. I promise you will be sent straight to the South when you sink your teeth into these warm, flavorful pillows of love!

1 1/4 pound of unpeeled, medium sized fresh shrimp
6 cups water
1 cup all-purpose flour
1 teaspoon baking powder
1 teaspoon pepper
2 large eggs
1/4 cup light beer
1 medium onion minced
2 teaspoons of Louisiana hot sauce
5 garlic cloves minced
1/2 teaspoon dried thyme
Vegetable oil

Peel shrimp and devein if desired. Bring 6 cups of water to a boil; add shrimp and cook for 3 to 5 minutes or just until shrimp turns pink. Drain and rinse with cold water. Chill shrimp. Coarsely chop shrimp.

Beat flour and next 5 ingredients at medium speed with an electric mixer until smooth. Stir in shrimp, onion and next 3 ingredients. Cover and chill 2 hours. (Batter will be very wet.)

Pour oil to a depth of 1 1/2 inches into a Dutch oven; heat to 375°. Drop batter by rounded tablespoonfuls and fry in batches 4 to 5 minutes or until golden brown. Drain fritters on paper towels. Serve hot. Makes about 20 fritters.

Pickled Shrimp

3 quarts water
4 tablespoons Old Bay Seasoning, divided
2 large bay leaves, crumbled if dried, chopped if fresh, divided
6 large cloves garlic, lightly crushed and peeled, divided
1 large rib celery, including leafy top, thinly sliced
Salt
2 pounds of small to medium fresh shrimp
1 cup white wine vinegar
1/2 cup minced shallot or Vidalia onion
2 large lemons divided
2 to 3 tablespoons of extra virgin olive oil (optional)
4 to 6 fresh lettuce leaves
2 tablespoons chopped of flat-leaf parsley

In a large stainless steel or enameled pot, add 3 quarts of water. Add 2 tablespoons Old Bay Seasoning, 1 bay leaf, 3 garlic cloves, celery, and a handful of salt. Bring to a boil over medium-high heat. Reduce heat to medium and simmer for 10 minutes. Increase heat and add shrimp; cover and cook for 2 minutes. Drain well and rinse under cold running water to stop cooking. Peel and de-vein shrimp, place in a glass bowl.

In a saucepan, bring vinegar, shallot or onion, remaining 2 tablespoons Old Bay® Seasoning, remaining bay leaf and 3 garlic cloves to a full boil over medium-high heat. Reduce heat to low and simmer for 5 minutes. Turn off heat. Let mixture cool slightly and pour over shrimp. Using a zester, zest 1 lemon in strips. Add zest strips to shrimp mixture; squeeze juice of zested lemon into mixture through a strainer. Toss well and let cool completely.

Cover and marinate for at least 4 hours or as long as 24 hours. Shrimp will keep for up to 2 weeks refrigerated.

Shrimp Remoulade

I have always thought of this as a truly New Orleans dish. I can remember watching Mom open the plastic bag with ice and wet newspaper inside and I would become so excited because I knew something amazing would be created from the freshest of fresh Gulf Shrimp that I just LOVE. It was magic to watch her rinse and then, just like some sort of machine, begin de-heading, peeling, and deveining these soon to be delicious creatures. Shrimp Remoulade is both a beautiful AND delicious dish that makes me flash back to many magical meal preparations.

1 cup of chopped freshly cooked shrimp
½ cup catsup
¼ cup parsley
4 green onions
1 /2 teaspoon Louisiana hot sauce
1 teaspoon yellow mustard
1 cup mayo
2 cloves of garlic
½ cup chopped celery
1 large onion
1 teaspoon brown mustard
1 teaspoon Worcestershire® sauce

Additional 1 dozen large parboiled shrimp peeled
Mix all ingredients EXCEPT LARGE Shrimp in blender and serve over Large Shrimp and lettuce.

Shrimp Stuffed Mushrooms

2 packages of whole button mushrooms
2 ½ medium onions
1 stick of butter
1/3 cup olive oil
5 sticks of celery
4 cloves garlic finely chopped
1 cup French cut green beans cooked
3 tablespoons fresh parsley
1 cup Parmesan cheese
1 cup bread crumbs
1 pound freshly cooked shrimp chopped fine

Finely chop all ingredients except the mushroom stems (go ahead and toss these or make something else with them). Sauté all ingredients except for shrimp, cheese, and bread crumbs for 5 minutes. Then add shrimp for 3 additional minutes. Remove from heat and stir in cheese and bread crumbs. Stuff into mushroom caps and sprinkle more Parmesan cheese over top. Bake in covered glass baking dish for 30 minutes at 300 degrees.

Hint – I often cook my stuffing a day or two before and then stuff the mushrooms, refrigerate covered and then bake on the evening of the event.

Crab Stuffed Mushrooms

I am a pushover for finger food. I am an especially easy target for finger food with good flavors. I think it is why I am in love with the stuffed mushroom. If you can make it a moist mixture with good flavors you can shoe it into a mushroom cap! I love crabmeat, chopped cooked shrimp or even chopped scallops in these. I have even been known to stuff mushrooms with bleu cheese and bacon. So let's start here and see where we can make it go.

2 packages of whole button mushrooms
2 ½ medium onions
1 stick of butter
1/3 cup olive oil
5 sticks of celery
1 head of garlic
3 tablespoons fresh parsley
1 cup Parmesan cheese
1 cup bread crumbs
1 pound crabmeat - jumbo lump or high quality claw meat

Finely chop all ingredients except the mushroom stems. Sauté all ingredients except for crabmeat, cheese, and bread crumbs for 5 minutes. Then add crabmeat for 5 additional minutes. Remove from heat and stir in cheese and bread crumbs. Stuff into mushroom caps and sprinkle more Parmesan cheese over top. Bake in covered glass baking dish for 30 minutes at 300 degrees.

Just like the shrimp stuffed mushrooms, I often make my stuffing the day before and then stuff and bake on the evening of the event.

Stuffed Artichokes

Now this is a shout out to my Aunt Gwen – not really my aunt but as close to being one as possible.

Trim the artichoke leaves and cut off the very top and the bottom stem so that the artichoke can sit flat. Steam in a covered pan over medium heat in about one inch of water until you can remove leaves easily. This usually takes 30 to 45 minutes depending on your artichoke. Let them cool completely before trying to stuff.

- ½ pound of butter (2 sticks)
- ½ cup olive oil
- 3 medium onions
- 5 sticks of celery
- 2 whole heads of garlic not toes
- 1 bunch of fresh parsley
- 3 cans of French style green beans

Throw all ingredients above except the green beans in food processor, mix away. Drain the green beans and add the seasonings such as salt and black pepper to taste. Add one regular sized can of Parmesan cheese and now add bread crumbs until you like the consistency. I usually add about half a can or more. Let the stuffing cool and stuff the artichoke.

Hint you can actually freeze this or keep in the refrigerator for a few days.

Spinach Shells

1 pound chopped spinach thawed and drained
½ medium onion finely chopped
5 cloves garlic finely chopped
2 tablespoons butter
4 ounces cream cheese softened
1 egg
1 package puffed pastry shells

Sauté spinach and onion in 2 tablespoons butter for 3 minutes. Add garlic and sauté for an additional 5 minutes. Remove from heat and let rest and cool for 5 minutes. Stir in softened cream cheese and set aside for additional 5 minutes. Beat egg in separate dish and add into cooled mixture. Set aside.

Take unbaked shells and spoon in mixture. Follow baking instructions for the shells and then remove from oven and serve!

Meaty Cheese Logs

3 8 ounce cream cheese
1 can black olives
1 8 ounce jar dried beef OR 12 ounces FINELY CHOPPED salami depending on your preference for the meat flavor
1 8 ounce jar mushrooms chopped
1 bunch of green onions chopped (do not use white part)
2 teaspoons Tony Chachere's Creole Seasoning
¾ teaspoon accent
1 ½ cups chopped pecans

In a large bowl mix cheese, accent, olives, green onion, mushrooms dried beef...Use hands (preferably washed hands). Form logs or rolls and then roll each log in nuts.

Refrigerate 1 hour and serve.

Soups

I have gotten a whole heap of grief on this one. I now live in South Florida, I don't make soups as often as I would like. I find that when the temperature hits 60, I start breaking everything out to make soup for the cold night here. It's amazing how 60 degrees is now cold. Soups are wonderful to prepare but even better to eat as leftovers in the fridge or even make individual containers for the freezer. When you don't have time to make a magical meal, you can just defrost one. Soups are a time to be creative. Using vegetable, chicken and beef stocks are great ways to create a base of the soup you want. Experiment with flavors that you like. Be bold, get creative and most of all have fun. Soups are fast and fun ways to use herbs and vegetables that you like to make a warm heart and warm should no matter what mixture you try. The following are some of my favorites with a variety of flavors and textures, so dig in and enjoy!

Maw's & Paw's House

A Whole Heap Of Goodness ● ● ● ● ● ● ● ● ● ● ●

Artichoke Soup

½ cup butter
1 large yellow onion chopped
1 bunch onion tops chopped
2 cloves garlic chopped
2 tablespoons fresh parsley chopped
2 (1 pound) cans artichoke hearts
1 cup water
1 can cream of mushroom soup 10 ½ oz can
1 bay leaf
2 cups of water
1 can of Pet® milk
Salt and pepper to taste

Melt butter in Dutch oven, and add onions cook till transparent, add garlic and parsley, cook for 2 to 3 minutes. Add drained artichoke hearts and cook for a few minutes and then add cream of mushroom soup and bay leaf. Cook for 10 minutes, then add salt and pepper to taste. Finally, add Pet® milk very slowly and then add water till you have your desired consistency.

Roasted Asparagus, Garlic and Potato Soup

Yum Yum and Yum again! Originally, I was not convinced I would like this soup….Oh who am I kidding, I love ANYTHING with garlic! I really enjoy this soup. The flavors are just awesome.

6 to 8 cloves of garlic
1 ¼ pound asparagus
2 cups of peeled and sliced gold potatoes
1 large Vidalia onion cut into 6 to 8 wedges
1 ½ tablespoons olive oil
½ teaspoon salt
½ teaspoon coarsely ground black pepper
3 cups chicken broth
6 ounces Greek yogurt
1 teaspoon lemon juice
1 bay leaf

Now before we get started – When I buy asparagus, I immediately cut the bottom by about ½ inch when I get home, place them in a glass with about an inch of water and refrigerate them. This keeps them fresh. Now let's get started. Once you remove these asparagus from the refrigerator cut them into about 1 inch pieces. You should have 3 cups more or less. Now in a large bowl toss the peeled and diced potatoes, asparagus, onion, olive oil, salt and pepper. Place whole cloves of garlic in a foil pouch with 1 teaspoon of water inside.

Spread veggies onto a high rimmed baking pan and bake on 375 for 35 to 45 minutes or until potatoes and asparagus are tender. Be sure to include the garlic pack in the oven at the same time for the same duration. Remove from oven and open foil packet and toss garlic in with veggies and let cool for about 10 minutes.

Transfer half of the roasted vegetables into a blender along with 1 ½ cups of the broth and blend until smooth. Pour mixture into small pot. Drop bay leaf into saucepan with mixture. Add last of roasted vegetables into blender with last 1 ½ cups of broth and pour into pot and warm over medium heat.

Your Own Ideas

Whisk yogurt and lemon juice into mixture and add the salt and pepper to taste.

Make it special – I have a tendency to cook bacon and crumble pieces over the top of this soup to add a bit more heartiness to the roasted flavors in the soup.

Baked Potato Soup

Now here is a soup that makes my toes curl. There are so many different ways to make baked potato soup that you can really let your imagination soar! The following recipe is what I often use as my base and the garnish ingredients are what you can really use to get creative. Now New Orleans winters are damp as all get out. Although it may only be 30 degrees, it just seems to go right through you. Make the soup your own and realize that there is nothing better on a cold nasty winter day than this amazing rib sticking soup!

4 large baking potatoes, unpeeled but well-scrubbed
3 tablespoons butter
1 ½ medium onions chopped
1 clove garlic chopped
Olive oil for rubbing potatoes
3 tablespoons flour
1 cup chicken stock
2 cups of half and half
1 ½ tablespoons fresh chopped parsley

Scrub potatoes well and rub with olive oil and then salt whole potatoes well. Bake in oven on 375 for 50 to 60 minutes or until tender. Remove from oven and let potatoes cool till warm or room temperature. Coarsely chop potatoes. Melt butter in saucepan over medium heat and add onions. Sauté until translucent but not browned. Add flour and stir constantly until it is a golden in color (not brown). Congratulations you have just prepared a roux!!! Now add chicken stock and bring mixture to a boil.

You should be stirring the mixture constantly until it is smooth and thickened. Now add potatoes, half and half and parsley. Mix well over medium heat for another 10 minutes. Do NOT allow the mixture to come to a boil as this will curdle your milk.

FUN PART – Now to add your own whole heap of special. You can blend the soup for a thicker creamier texture or leave it as it is. For adding zing to your soup and to make it your own, top with any of the following and feel free to mix and match your favorites!

Sour cream
Chopped chives
Crumbled cooked bacon
Shredded cheddar cheese
Blue cheese crumbles
Shredded pepper jack cheese
Chopped scallions
Chopped roasted garlic
Roasted asparagus
Cube left over grilled chicken

Your options are limitless!

Your Favorites

Cream of Carrot Soup

This recipe reminds me of my cousin Lisa. For Thanksgiving she started bringing this delicious treat. For me, nothing says Thanksgiving like a beautiful rich orange colored soup. For a warmth that will warm your soul on even the coldest of days like a conversation with my sweet cousin Lisa this soup is the way to **go.**

1 stick (8 ounce) butter
1/2 cup plus 1 tablespoon all-purpose flour
2 1/2 cups coarsely chopped carrots
2 quarts chicken stock
6 ounces heavy cream
Salt, pepper and Louisiana hot sauce to taste

Hint: Garnish with fresh chopped parsley or chives. If you want this soup to be even richer a small dollop of sour cream on top will do it. I often serve this soup with oven toasted baguette slices.

Melt the butter in a large saucepan over medium heat and add the flour. Whisk for 3 to 4 minutes. Add the carrots and cook, stirring often for 3 minutes. Slowly add the stock whisking and simmer until the carrots are just tender, about 20 minutes. Add the cream and simmer for about 5 minutes. Season to taste. Eat it as is or blend it down to your desired consistency.

Carrot and Ginger Soup

This is often a spring favorite of mine! The ginger gives a flavor that just screams out that spring is near. The color is fantastic and looks great on a table.

5 tablespoons of olive oil
1 large onion finely chopped
¼ cup peeled and finely chopped fresh ginger
6 cups of chicken stock
2 pounds of carrots peeled and sliced
1 tablespoon of sugar
1 ½ cups of half and half
¼ cup flour
¼ teaspoon of ground cinnamon
Salt and pepper to your liking

Warm 2 of the 5 tablespoons of olive oil in a large sauce pan and sauté onion and ginger root until the onion is translucent and golden but NOT browned. Add carrots, chicken stock and sugar cover and simmer for 35 minutes.

Remove mixture from stove top and let cool for 15 minutes and then pour into blender or food processor in batches and puree. Optional – Strain mixture. Rinse and dry sauce pan and add the last 3 tablespoons of olive oil heating on medium. Stir in flour and cook until bubbly. Do not brown. Slowly add carrot mixture stirring constantly until well blended. Add half and half and stir constantly over medium heat careful not to boil as you will curdle the half and half. Continue to heat over medium/low for 5 to 10 minutes. Season with cinnamon and add salt and pepper to taste and serve.

Chicken Noodle Soup

1 (3 1/2 to 4 pound broiler fryer, halved
1 large onion, quartered
1 turnip, peeled and halved
1 ¼ teaspoons salt
1/4 teaspoon dried tarragon
3 cups chicken broth
1 large onion chopped
2 carrots, scraped and sliced
1/2 teaspoon pepper

2 stalks celery, halved
1 carrot, scraped and halved
2 cloves garlic, crushed
3/4 teaspoon pepper
4 cups water
4 ounces medium egg noodles, uncooked
2 stalks celery, sliced
1/2 teaspoon salt
1/4 teaspoon tarragon

Combine chicken and next 10 ingredients in a large Dutch oven and bring mixture to a boil over high heat. Reduce heat; cook for 45 minutes until chicken is tender. Remove chicken from broth; set broth mixture aside. Pour broth mixture through a wire mesh strainer into a large bowl; discard cooked vegetables. Remove and discard fat from broth; return broth to Dutch oven.

Cook noodles according to package directions omitting salt and fat, drain and set aside. Add chopped onion, sliced celery and carrots to chicken broth; bring to a boil over high heat. Reduce heat; simmer 15 minutes. Stir in chopped chicken and noodles; add ½ teaspoon salt and remaining ingredients. Cook until thoroughly heated. Makes 10 cups.

Cauliflower and Cheddar Soup

Those who know me or someone like me know that I LOVE color. I am not a fan of food that looks too bland or white. This, however, is one for the records. I HATED cauliflower as a child and would tend to eat it solely by accident if my mom had covered it in heaps of cheese. So I found a way to combine the two and make a thick creamy dish for winter.

2 tablespoons of olive oil
1 medium to large onion chopped
About 2 ½ pounds of cauliflower cut into flowerets
5 cups of chicken broth
2 cups of heavy cream
2 teaspoons salt
Ground pepper to taste
10 ounces shredded white cheddar

Warm oil on medium to high and add onion. Sauté till translucent and then add florets of cauliflower and cook till a slight golden brown about 5 to 7 minutes. Add broth, cream, salt and pepper. Bring to a boil and then lower to simmer and cover and cook for about 15 minutes stirring frequently.

Remove from heat and let cool 1 to 3 minutes and add to blender or food processor in batches and puree. Once all is pureed place back into pot and on LOW add cheese and stir until well mixed. Ladle into bowls and serve.

Angie's Corn and Crab Chowder

My cousin Angie is a hoot! She is a Fabulous cook and every time I turn around she is offering up a new recipe to try. I always love talking to her because we can talk nonstop about food and food recipe ideas. She is daring and fun in the kitchen and remains an inspiration to me to never be afraid to try something new. Let's face it, if you are trying something new and you are cooking for yourself why not be bold. It often is fun and exciting to see what you can come up with. Angie, I love you and this is the first of a few of yours that I have mixed up a bit!

1 tablespoon butter
1 large onion chopped
14.5 ounce can of chicken broth
1 standard package frozen niblets
2 small packs of frozen niblets in sauce
1 pound whole lump crabmeat
1 pint half and half
2 tablespoons fresh parsley chopped

Sauté onion in butter. Pour the large bag of frozen corn with the chicken broth into the blender and puree. Pour puree into large pot with the sautéing onion and cook on medium to low heat for 5 minutes. Add 2 packages of niblets in sauce to mixture and cook additional 10 to 15 minutes. Add crabmeat, half and half and cook additional 10 minutes and then add parsley, salt and pepper to taste. Serve, garnish with fresh chopped parsley or chives and enjoy.

My cousins Angie, Jaime, & Michel

Mom's French Onion Soup

I am mad about French Onion Soup!!! I think I fell in love with this tasty treat when I was much younger for one reason and one reason only, CHEESE. To this day it is my favorite part of this delectable dish. I often find myself saving the cheese until the very end and savoring every last toasted, gooey bite. I can remember no matter what restaurant we went to, I would try and convince mom and dad to let me order this. There was something magical about the toasted cheese that bubbled and browned and the piping hot, savory broth that lay underneath it. Eating this as a child was like opening a food present – magical.

10 medium yellow onions thinly sliced
5 cups water
2 twelve ounce cans of beer
2 tablespoons Worcestershire® sauce
3 tablespoons chopped parsley
9 beef flavored bouillon cubes
2 or 3 cloves of garlic chopped
½ teaspoon dry mustard
½ teaspoon dill
½ teaspoon celery seed
¼ teaspoon marjoram
1 bay leaf
Salt and ground white pepper to taste

Separate onions and cook in large Dutch oven with butter on medium heat for 25 to 30 minutes stirring frequently. Add the sherry and cook for 5 minutes. Add remaining ingredients and bring to a boil, then cover and reduce to simmer for 1 hour.

This freezes beautifully.

Your Favorites

Crawfish Chowder

1 stick of butter
1 large onion chopped
3 or 4 cloves of garlic
1 can cream of mushroom soup
1 can cream of celery soup
1 ½ can of milk – measured out in the soup cans
1 pound Mexican Velveeta®
1 XX ounce bag of chopped broccoli cooked and drained
1 pound of crawfish in fat
Salt and pepper to taste

Melt butter and sauté onion and garlic for 3 to 5 minutes. Add soups and milk and mix thoroughly. Add cheese and mix until well melted. Simmer on low to medium until thoroughly heated. Add broccoli and stir gently. Add crawfish tails and mix well. Continue on low to medium for 10 to 12 more minutes. Garnish with chopped Green onion, parsley or chives and serve.

Southern Sweet Potato Soup

2 ½ tablespoons butter
1 cup finely chopped Vidalia onion
1/3 cup finely chopped green bell pepper
2 tablespoons all purpose flour
1 ½ teaspoons salt
2 cups of chicken broth
1 teaspoon Louisiana hot sauce

2 cups cooked and mashed sweet potatoes
2 cups of milk
2 teaspoons parsley
1 teaspoon freshly sliced ginger or ½ teaspoon ground ginger
Ground nutmeg
Finely chopped green onion or chives

Melt butter and sauté onions and peppers on medium heat until onions are translucent – 3 or 4 minutes. Add flour and salt and stir well. Add broth, sweet potatoes, hot sauce and milk, stir constantly until well blended and slightly thickened. Serve warm in bowls and garnish with chopped green onion or chives and a bit of ground nutmeg! A warm beautifully orange treat!

Tortilla Soup with Shrimp and Avocado

1 tablespoon olive oil
1 cup pre-chopped onion
1/3 cup pre-chopped celery
1/3 cup chopped carrot
1 tablespoon minced chipotle chile, canned in adobo sauce
1 teaspoon ground cumin
1 teaspoon chili powder
2 teaspoons minced garlic
4 cups fat-free, lower sodium chicken broth
1 (15 ounce) can white hominy, rinsed and drained
1 (15 ounce) can no-salt added fire-roasted diced tomatoes, undrained.
12 ounces peeled and de-veined medium shrimp
1 tablespoon fresh lime
1/8 teaspoon salt
1/2 cup lightly crushed baked tortilla chips (about 1 ounce)
1 cup diced avocado (about 1/2 pound)
2 tablespoons fresh cilantro leaves (optional)

I generally do not use a stock pot for this soup as things just don't seem to cook right. I tend to use the Dutch oven mom gave me. Add oil to pan; swirl to coat. Add onion and next 6 ingredients (through garlic). Cook 6 minutes or until carrot is crisp-tender, stirring occasionally. Add broth, hominy and tomatoes; bring to a boil. Cover and cook 6 minutes; stirring occasionally. Add shrimp; cook 2 minutes or until shrimp are done.

Remove from heat; stir in LIME juice and salt. Divide shrimp mixture evenly among 4 bowls; top evenly with chips and avocado. Garnish with cilantro, if desired.

Taco Soup

- 1 whole roasted Chicken cut up
- 2 cans red kidney beans drained and rinsed
- 1 can black beans
- 1 can of Rotel®
- 1 can diced tomatoes
- 1 can of whole kernel corn in water
- 1 pack of taco seasoning mix

Combine all Ingredients and let simmer for 1 hour. I often then remove the cut up chicken and debone it and place the meat back into the soup. I often top this soup with a dollop of sour cream sprinkle grated cheddar or pepper jack cheese and then a clove of roasted garlic.

Tomato Basil Soup

- 4 cups tomatoes – when I am in a hurry I use 4 cups of canned whole tomatoes and crush them
- 4 cups of tomato juice – I sometimes use 2 cups spicy V-8® and 2 cups of regular V-8®
- 14 fresh basil leaves
- 1 cup of whipping cream
- ½ stick of unsalted butter
- ½ teaspoon cracked black pepper

Combine tomatoes and juice in a saucepan and simmer on low/medium for 30 minutes. Let cool for 15 to 20 minutes. Then place in blender or food processor in batches and puree with basil. Return the pureed mixture to saucepan and while on low heat add cream and butter stirring until all ingredients are well mixed. Stir in salt to taste and additional ground black pepper to taste. Garnish with fresh basil or small dollop of sour cream and serve with crusty French baguette.

Chicken Chili

I tried this at a friend's house while I was living in Omaha. It was about 2 degrees outside and there was about a foot of snow on the ground. I had never missed the warm South more than I did that day. I can remember going inside to a house that just smelled delicious. I think I had 3 bowls of her chili that day. I found this recipe about 3 years ago again and always have some on hand in the freezer when I am feeling cold. I have adapted it a few different ways over the last few years and it is yet another reason why I love chili. Feel free to play with your chili and make it wholly yours and of course have fun and Dig in!

1 whole chicken
2 tablespoons olive oil
1 large chopped onion
5 or 6 cloves of garlic finely chopped
3 cans of white beans
5 tomatillos husked stemmed and chopped
16 ounces frozen white corn
1 tablespoon cumin
2 tablespoons chili powder – I have at times added an extra half or even a whole tablespoon
1 tablespoon cayenne
1 teaspoon oregano
2 4 ounce cans of green chilies
2 cups of chicken broth
2 tablespoons lime juice
2 tablespoons of chopped fresh cilantro – if you do not like cilantro feel free to use fresh chopped parsley

Boil the chicken in enough water to fully cover it. Boil for 1 hour, save the broth and remove skin and debone chicken. Once deboned, cut chicken into chunks. Heat oil in a large pot and sauté onion and garlic until they turn a nice golden color. Add beans and heat. Now add all remaining ingredients except the parsley and lime juice. Add 3 cups of chicken broth. Simmer uncovered for an hour and a half to two hours. Add chicken broth as you see it evaporating out of chili to keep your desired consistency. Just before serving stir in lime juice and garnish with parsley or cilantro. I like to add sour cream or pepper jack cheese.

Your Favorites

Vegetarian Chili

Ok I know most people cringe when they see a southerner talking crazy talk like this but yes, I have been known to make vegetarian chili. The recipe comes from one of my dear friends back in college. This is her recipe at heart...I just throw a whole heap of Chad at it.

2 medium purple onions chopped
5 cloves garlic chopped
2 medium green bell peppers chopped
3 tablespoons olive oil
1 can black beans drained and rinsed
1 can of kidney beans drained and rinsed
1 standard size container of tofu cut into ½ inch chunks
1 large can pureed tomatoes
1 tablespoon chopped green chilies.

Sauté your veggies in the olive oil till the onions are translucent then add remainder of ingredients.

Now add:

1 ½ teaspoon cumin
½ teaspoon nutmeg
2 ½ to 3 teaspoons chili powder
Salt and pepper to taste

Let this simmer for at least 45 minutes. I love to let this go for an hour to an hour and a half myself to really get those flavors penetrating.

White Turkey Chili

2 tablespoons olive oil
1 large Vidalia onion chopped
1 tablespoon ground cumin
6 to 8 cloves of garlic chopped
1 jalapeno seeded and chopped
3 7 ounce jars of fire roasted Anaheim chilies chopped
4 to 4 ½ cups chicken stock
1 ¼ pounds cooked turkey
3 15 ounce can of cannellini or white beans drained and rinsed
2 tablespoons chopped fresh oregano
1/3 cup chopped parsley – I don't care for cilantro
1/3 cup cornmeal

Put oil in large sauté pan and add oil and sauté on medium heat until translucent. Add cumin, salt, pepper, garlic and jalapeno and sauté for another 2 minutes. Stir in canned or jarred chilies and 3 to 3 ½ cups of the chicken stock. Dump all into large crock pot and add turkey, beans, oregano and parsley. Mix cornmeal and ½ cup broth and then pour into crock pot. Cover crock pot and place on high for 3 to 3 ½ hours. Add more broth if necessary for desired thickness. Ladle out chili and serve with crushed tortilla chips on top, add shredded pepper jack cheese and a dollop of sour cream.

Thanksgiving 1981

Entrées & Sides

Sweet and Spicy Oven Barbecued Brisket

Now let's be honest, slow cooked brisket smells AMAZING and you just have to want to eat it. I can think over and over of the amazing smell floating throughout our house growing up and each and every time I think of this smell and meal I simply smile from ear to ear...and then notice I may be drooling. This is a very easy and delicious way to make a very yummy meal.

If you are not in the mood for the smoky chipotle peppers then use 2 tablespoons of Louisiana hot sauce. This is often great to serve when you want to sit and spend time with your company arrives and not have them in the kitchen with you. So sit a spell with your guests and when this comes out of the oven you are all sure to be salivating.

3 lb. trimmed brisket
1 tablespoon garlic powder
1/2 cup packed brown sugar
Sandwich, sesame hamburger or Hawaiian rolls

Salt and pepper
2 cups chipotle chunky salsa
1/2 cup Worcestershire® sauce

Season brisket with salt, pepper and garlic; place in a 3 quart shallow baking dish. Mix salsa, brown sugar and Worcestershire® sauce and spread over brisket. Cover and refrigerate overnight.

Bake covered at 300° for 4 ½ to 5 hours or until tender. Slice or shred brisket with a fork and serve with juices on rolls.

Boulette Fricasse - From Maw to Nanny to Me!!!

Here is another family favorite. Aunt Net, Nanny, is the hero on this recipe. I have LOVED this recipe my whole life. I rarely get home to Louisiana and often miss it terribly. I know that there is a staple every Christmas Christmas day is now held at my cousin's home. Everyone brings food and every year I know that Nanny will be making boulette fricassee. This meaty meatball and brown gravy dish makes me grin from ear to ear. Even before we officially 'start' the meal I am always sure to be hovering over the large Dutch oven sampling these delicious morsels. I am always going to have 2 or 3 servings of this dish no matter what other foods are around. My cousin Judd and I attack these until we are dizzy or just feel miserable because we have eaten so much. There always seems to be a silent, or not so silent discussion of who is eating more of these meatballs with rich gravy. Over the last 3 or 4 years we have gotten more and more vocal about who is eating how much. It's all love fun and games...as long as he leaves me some to take home!

My favorite part of this whole tradition is that Nanny always sneaks me a frozen container of boulettes and a bit of gravy that I am sure to bring home to Florida. I often watch this container in my freezer and exert the strongest of will power in order to resist eating this treat almost immediately. If all goes well and I am able to control myself, I wait until my birthday, March 4, and I thaw it out and enjoy it all over again and think of my Nanny on my birthday. I have been asked why I simply don't whip up a bath all of my own for my birthday. The answer is simple, It's not Nanny's. When it is the fricassee that comes from her and from her kitchen, it is all the more special. Her love becomes closer and the hundreds of miles that lie between us just seem to melt away. These are the things that make life a Whole Heap of Special!

Boulette Fricasse
(Continued)

2 pounds of ground beef
½ pound ground pork
4 cloves of garlic
½ onion finely chopped
½ green bell pepper finely chopped
1 egg
1/3 bunch of finely chopped parsley
4 or 5 green onions chopped
Salt and pepper to taste

Mix all above ingredients and make into small meatballs (cocktail size) and fry in small amount of olive oil, turning constantly.

Now to prepare the Fricasse:

1 cup of roux
1 onion finely chopped
½ green bell pepper finely chopped
1 ½ quarts of water
2/3 finely chopped parsley
6 green onions finely chopped

In a thick Dutch oven mix all ingredients and add meatballs. Bring to a boil and then reduce to a simmer. Simmer for 45 minutes and then continue to simmer until you have your desired consistency. Always remember it is easier to thin this grave youth rather than thicken it up. To thin out, add water. To thicken gravy, add roux.

Serve this delicious dish over prepared white rice.

Creamy Artichoke Spinach and Goat Cheese Casserole

Once again, we get to use one of my favorite ingredients – CHEESE! This time we get to use goat cheese. Goat cheese seems to be an ingredient that I have found people to be afraid of. There is nothing to fear with using goat cheese andhis mouth-watering casserole is a wonderful place to start. This casserole is creamy and makes my mouth water just thinking about it. I have done so many adaptations of this recipe that it is not even funny. I have even turned it into a type of mac and cheese. All in all, the following is a great place to open your eyes to goat cheese. Never forget, artichokes and spinach are a delicious combination so go for it and then Dig in! I often get the cheese varities from one of my favorite stores here in Fort Lauderdale that must have close to 2 dozen different types of goat's cheese and ridiculously amazing boutique wines!

2 teaspoons olive oil
2 medium to large shallots chopped
4 cloves of garlic chopped
18 to 24 ounces of marinated artichoke hearts chopped
2 cups fresh spinach roughly chopped
½ teaspoon herbs de Provence
1 ¾ cups milk
½ teaspoon ground black pepper
¼ to ½ teaspoon salt
4 large eggs
½ cup of grated Parmigiano-Reggiano cheese
5 cups cubed white loaf bead (usually from your local grocery store's bakery)
1 ¼ cups crumbled goat cheese
Pam® non-stick spray

Place olive oil in large sauté pan. Throw in shallots and sauté on medium for 2 ½ to 3 minutes until shallots are becoming translucent. Toss in garlic and artichoke hearts and cook until artichoke hearts begin to brown (usually 8 to 10 minutes). Remove from heat and toss spinach and mix well; this should wilt your spinach. Now stir in herbs de Provence and set aside for 10 to 12 minutes.

Combine milk, salt, pepper, eggs and whisk briskly in a large mixing bowl. Add cheese and stir gently. Add bead and stir gently again. Finally, stir in the spinach and artichoke mixture and set aside for 20 minutes.

Spray a medium casserole dish with Pam®, (8x8, 11x7 or round) spoon out half of bread mix then sprinkle with ½ of goat cheese. Spoon out remaining bread mixture followed by the remaining goat cheese on top. Bake at 375° for about 45 to 50 minutes or until top is golden brown and the casserole is bubbly.

Hint – to make this amazing casserole more hearty feel free to add 1 ½ to 2 cups of cut up grilled chicken breast to the bread mixture.

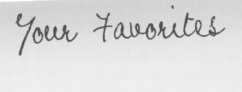

Your Favorites

Cheesy Covered Cauliflower

OK I out-and-out stole this one from our friend David. We had this awesome side dish as an appetizer one evening at his home. It is simple and let's face it – how can you go wrong with cheese. You will laugh when you watch the faces on your guests when you are ready to serve this because it can be presented in a variety of ways and it can really be beautiful!

1 head of cauliflower
1 jar of seed mustard
3 tablespoons salt
Your favorite cheese block

Cut very bottom of cauliflower stem off so that the head will sit upright and fairly level. Place salt into large pot and add water to point of being able to place head of cauliflower in and have it cover the head completely. Boil water and then place in cauliflower. Boil cauliflower for 7 minutes and remove from pot and place into oven safe dish. Cover head of cauliflower with seed mustard and thenn cover mustard with large slices of cheese. Bake in oven on 400 for 5 to 7 minutes or until cheese melts and just begins to brown. Remove, slice and serve!

Baked Fusilli with Lemon and Spinach

10 ounces of Fuseli Pasta
1 tablespoon olive oil
1/3 cup flour
2 ½ cups milk
1 cup grated Parmesan cheese
½ teaspoon ground black pepper
1 cup panko bread crumbs

6 ounces fresh baby spinach
4 cups of chopped onion
6 cloves garlic chopped finely
½ cup dry white wine
¾ - 1 teaspoon salt
½ teaspoon grated lemon rind
Pam® non-stick spray

Cook Fuseli in boiling water for about 8 minutes so that it is NOT quite al dente. Remove from stove toss in spinach and allow to wilt then drain. Heat sauté pan over medium heat and add olive oil and throw in onion and allow to brown a bit past translucent (this should take about 15 minutes). Add flour and garlic stirring constantly. Gradually add milk and wine and continue to cook until sauce begins to boil and thicken. Finally stir in half of cheese and all of the lemon and salt. Remove from heat and add pepper and then mix in pasta mixture. Spoon pasta into a large casserole pan that you have coated with Pam. Sprinkle half of bread crumbs followed by remaining cheese then top with last of bread crumbs. Place dish in oven on 350 and bake for 50 to 55 minutes, until the dish is browned and bubbly. Remove from oven and serve.

Hint – I sometimes add cooked grilled lemon chicken to this in order to make it a bit more substantial and to have a bit more meat!

BBQ Shrimp

This is not necessarily for the super health conscious. I drool when I even think about this recipe! I can just picture it. Hot shrimp, warm French bread and the juice dripping down the corner of my mouth, this is a New Orleans favorite . Anyone who is from New Orleans has a BBQ Shrimp recipe or story. It is a local favorite and a recipe that has as many variations as the city has residents. I promise you this is a good version and you will not be disappointed. I can already see myself sitting on momma's back patio with a really cold beer and a bowl of this delicious masterpiece. As a child I remember watching mom and dad peel the flavor filled shells off of the shrimp while enjoying the breeze from the fan on the back patio. And even now I smile because I watch as Jeff eagerly awaits these spicy morsels arrival from the oven while he paces eagerly back and forth across mom's kitchen ready to "taste" the first one out of the oven. Yes, be sure to serve this in a bowl because half of the joy is sopping up the juice with that fresh French bread. O MY!

2 pounds large raw shrimp
1 ½ sticks butter
1/3 cup olive oil
4 large sticks of rosemary or 2 tablespoons of dried
1 ½ tablespoons whole black peppercorn
2 lemons sliced
10 cloves of garlic sliced
1 tablespoon dried basil
1 tablespoon dried oregano
1 lemon to squeeze

Place shrimp in 9x12 pan. Squeeze ½ lemon in bowl and mix softened butter and olive oil and add spices and mix well. Spoon mixture over shrimp in pan. Lay rosemary stalks over the top of the shrimp. Place sliced lemons over the top of shrimp and cover with foil. Place pan in refrigerator for at least 2 hours. When ready to bake remove pan from refrigerator for 15 to 20 minutes before baking. Preheat oven to 400 degrees leave shrimp covered and bake for 7 to 8 minutes and then remove and stir. Recover pan and bake for 5 to 7 minutes more remove from oven.

Serve in a bowl with the juice and shrimp. Accompany this dish with fresh French bread and use it for dipping into sauce!

Chicken and Sundried Tomatoes

This is one amazing recipe. This is an uncomplicated and more importantly DELICIOUS recipe. A true mix of flavors and color I have a tendency to throw in a spare piece of red pepper or yellow pepper for a touch of extra sweetness and color. IF you want to make this dish a tad on the healthier side, use fat free half and half instead of heavy cream. But let face it, I prefer the heavy cream! Hahahaha!!!

1 to 1 ½ cups chicken breast diced
2 ½ tablespoons olive oil
1 large shallot OR 2 tablespoons diced onion
1 tablespoon Dijon mustard
2/3 cup heavy cream
2 tablespoons white wine
1 or 2 tablespoons tarragon depending on your taste for it
1 cup of sun dried tomatoes (bagged, not the kind in oil)

Soften tomatoes by soaking in boiling water for 5 minutes then drain, cut into small strips and set aside.

In skillet heat oil and sauté the chicken for 4 to 5 minutes. Using slotted spoon, remove chicken and place on platter. Place onion into skillet and sauté for 1 minute.

Put mustard, cream, wine, tarragon, and tomatoes into bowl and mix well. Add the mixture to the skillet with onions and simmer until desired thickness.

Add chicken to the skillet and simmer only until all heated and serve over any kind of cooked pasta you like.

Black Eyed Peas

3 cups of dry black eye peas
6 cups of water
Ham to season or can used cooked bacon for flavor
1 ¼ cups chopped Vidalia onion if ya got em
1 cup green peppers chopped
4 cloves of garlic...or 5 if you like chopped
2 bay leaves
Salt and pepper to taste
(OPTIONAL – can of stewed tomatoes)

Your Favorites

Sort peas and place in large Dutch oven. You should have at least 2 inches of water ABOVE the peas. Soak for at LEAST 2 hours. HINT you can even soak these overnight and it will cut the cook time in HALF.

Drain water and return peas to pot. Add 6 cups of water and the next 5 ingredients and bring to a boil. Then cover and reduce to a low simmer for about 45 minutes to an hour stirring occasionally.

If you decided to add tomatoes add after the 45 min and cook another 15 minutes or until beans are soft.

Bread and Butter Pickles

Look out everyone this is another nod to Maw! I must admit, I MISS this so much. I can remember walking into her little laundry area with it's wall to wall cabinets that Paw had built himself and standing there in awe looking at the rows and rows of jars with color after color of jarred deliciousness. There were jars of canned figs that I LOVED to mix with peanut butter, jars of canned pears from her yard turned pink by the couple of maraschino cherries she would drop in, and then of course the ultimate jar...her bread and butter pickles! The amazing gems have been a love of mine for decades. I would eat them straight from the jar. However, my ultimate use of these pickles was to add them to a good old fashioned chicken and sausage gumbo with a spoonful of maw's bread and butter pickle juice and several of these amazing little juicy morsels.

1 gallon of cucumbers sliced thin
2 large yellow onions Vidalia if you can get them
2 green peppers sliced
½ cup salt
2 trays of ice about 4 cups
5 cups of vinegar
5 cups of sugar
½ teaspoons turmeric
½ teaspoon ground cloves
2 tablespoons mustard seed
1 teaspoon celery seed

Put cucumbers, onions, pepper in large container. Sprinkle Salt on top. Cover with ice and let stand for 3 hours – Drain well...Add remaining ingredients to cucumber and place over heat, turning until just BEFORE boiling. Place in HOT jars ¾ full with pickles then fill remaining space with juice. Let stand for minimum of 48 hours before serving.

Cheesy Potatoes

This is your chance! Go wild, experiment, be bold. I have used over 20 different types of cheese in this recipe. If you are going to embark on the A whole heap of goodness experience, then use the below recipe and mix it up. The best way to do this is to experiment with the cheese. Replace the cheddar with whatever you like. If you don't like the outcome, which I doubt, then start over and for heaven's sake have some fun!

12 medium new potatoes unpeeled and cut into cubes
½ cup melted butter
¼ teaspoon ground black or white pepper
1 cup fully cooked chopped bacon
2 cups sharp or extra sharp grated cheddar cheese
¼ cup chopped fresh parsley

Cover potatoes with salted water and bring to a boil. Reduce heat and simmer for an additional 15 minutes or until tender. Drain potatoes and let cool slightly. Stir in butter and pepper and toss a bit.

Spoon half of the potato mixture into a lightly greased 3 qt casserole dish top with half of the bacon and cheese. Repeat and then Bake at 350 degrees for 20 minutes or until bubbly. Garnish with the parsley and serve to very happy guests or family.

Broccoli Rice

Chris & Michel

This recipe has been a part of Thanks-givings and Christmases for years and years. It has become so popular with a few of my cousins that my mother often must triple the recipe for our large family gatherings. Mom has threatened a few times to not make this dish and there has been all but a general revolt. In addition to the tripled recipe Mom often makes separate batch to split to my cousins Michelle and Kristin because they always beg for extra to take home because no matter how much mom makes the dish is ALWAYS gone by the end of the day. The recipe is simple and often can be prepared very quickly and makes a great dish to bring to a "pot luck" or church event. I always have the simple ingredients in the freezer and the pantry so I can prepare this at a moment's notice and still look as if I have worked tirelessly in honor of an event or unexpected guests. I think this is a great comfort food and always takes me back to time with my extended family and the fun that these times bring.

1 package chopped frozen broccoli
1 cup cooked rice
1 can condensed cream of mushroom soup
1 ½ sticks butter
1 small package slivered almonds
1 8 ounce jar of Cheese Whiz®

Melt butter add thawed broccoli – DO NOT BOIL – simmer till tender (usually about 5 minutes).

Add soup, cooked rice, almonds and half of the cheese whiz and mix well. Add salt and pepper to taste. Add remaining cheese whiz to top of casserole and cover – microwave till topped cheese whiz starts to melt and serve.....

This can be done days ahead of time and re-heated either in the oven under 300 degrees or in the microwave.

Broccoli Casserole

2 packages of frozen chopped broccoli cooked
¼ cup chopped onions
6 teaspoons butter
2 teaspoons flour
½ cup bread crumbs
1/ cup water
1 8 ounce Cheese Whiz®
3 eggs

Sauté onions in 4 teaspoons of butter, stir in flour, and add water. Cook until thick; mix in cheese whiz and cooked broccoli and the beaten eggs. Top the casserole with the bread crumbs and the remaining butter.

Bake at 350° for 45 minutes to an hour.

Make It
Your Own

Crazy Cajun Fettuccini

This recipe is RICH! I love it and remember the reaction I got the first time I made this recipe for friends in Saint Louis. They went wild. I got this from My Nanny – that's godmother to any of you who don't know. She is another ridiculously amazing cook in the family. There are so many stories and about her that it can make you dizzy. To this day, she calls me Jaws because of my voracious appetite and the way in which I can just attack food. There are few people that can make me smile and laugh the way she does. I can think of no better way to let her know how much I love and appreciate her than to just say it and to include some of my favorite recipes of hers that make me smile and leave me in awe every time I cook them. Every time I turn around she has whipped up something else to make my head spin. I am so darned lucky to have her as my nanny.

1 ½ sticks of butter
3 medium yellow onions chopped
2 medium green onions chopped
3 cloves of garlic chopped 4 cloves if you are me
2 tablespoons of jalapeno pepper chopped fine
¼ teaspoon cayenne pepper
½ teaspoon Louisiana hot sauce
¼ cup of all purpose flour
½ bunch fresh parsley – about 4 tablespoons
1 pint of half and half
1 ounce of lemon juice – fresh is best folks
1 pound Velveeta® cheese cubed
3 pounds shrimp or crawfish tails
1 pound crabmeat
1 pound fettuccine noodles

Use a 12 quart roaster – on medium fire melt butter and sauté onions bell pepper, garlic, and jalapenos for about 15 minutes. Add salt to taste and the cayenne pepper and Louisiana Hot Sauce – this is the crazy Cajun part...Add flour slowly stirring constantly. Cook for about 10 minutes. Add fresh parsley and allow to soften mixture while stirring. Add half and half, lemon juice, and cheese.

Continue to stir until it has all become a well blended mixture.

Parboil shrimp or crawfish tails for about 3 minutes.

Add to mixture and allow to cook on LOW for additional 15 minutes. Stir in cooked noodles. Pour mixture into 4 quart OR larger casserole pan and garnish with parsley, thin sliced lemon and cheese.

a Whole Heap More Special

Crazed Chicken

2 ½ pounds chicken cooked and de-boned
1 box Uncle Ben's® long grain and wild rice cooked
1 can cream of celery coup
1 medium yellow onion chopped
1 2 ounce jar pimentos drained
1 cup mayo
1 8 ounce can of water chestnuts drained
16 ounces of French style green beans
Grated Parmesan cheese
Paprika a bit
Salt and pepper to taste
Dash or two of hot sauce

Mix all ingredients in a large bowl with the exception of the paprika and Parmesan cheese. Pour into a greased 9x13 baking dish and sprinkle with paprika and parmesan bake at 350° for 30 to 40 minutes.

***This can be made ahead of time and frozen before you decide to bake. Just make sure you allow time for it to thaw out before baking.

Carrot Jell-O® Salad

Ok I know what you are thinking...You are having some sort of odd flashback to some awful 60's ambrosia! But you would be wrong. This recipe is all Aunt Annie. It is no wonder how much it makes me smile when I think of her and food. Her creations were always good and more importantly, they were amazingly different dishes. Now that she is gone, I bring her back into my mind with a preparation of her fantastically fabulous and comforting dishes. I know it's kind of surprising but I like this even though it has no cheese or cream. This is an easy and yummy comfort dish. I love this in the summer to go along with BBQ. I love this dish in the winter because of its wonderful winter white color with the flecks of carrot and pineapple. I have had this as a side with pulled pork, as a wonderful brunch item and even as a delicious dessert. The key is the salt that really cuts the sweetness of this dish and makes it so darned yummy. Let's face it, it is almost healthy since it has fruit and carrots in it. Hahahaha. I know you will enjoy this one and make it your own. I can't ever make this one without flashing back to Aunt Annie's kitchen with the brick floors . The creations that she and Uncle Pat made always stirred my imagination because of their amazing colors, textures, and unique flavors. Think back I and I am sure you have similar food and family memories.

1 pack of lemon Jell-O®
1 cup boiling water
1 can crushed pineapple
¼ teaspoon salt
1 cup grated carrots
1 small container of Cool Whip®
½ cup chopped pecans (optional)

Open pineapple and drain juice into measuring cup and then add water until you have 1 cup liquid.

Add boiling water to lemon Jell-O®; add syrup/water mixture and salt. Put into refrigerator until it starts to jell then add remaining ingredients. Stir all together and place back in the refrigerator.

This is best if done the day or night before serving. Garnish with grated carrots and chopped pecans!

Chicken Fricassé

I am just a fanatic about fricassee. I was never the best at eating things that I was unsure of as a child but this dish just stuck with me and it was often my birthday dinner request . Nothing to me says home like a hot fricassee. This is Southern down home like no other. As all real old school southern dishs, it is inexpensive and gets better the longer you let it simmer. I have had many versions of fricassee so do not be afraid to make this delicious gravy dish your own. As with any roux based gravy, be sure to add the water as you go along rather than all at once. It is ALWAYS easier to thin out a fricassee than it is to thicken it up. I have a tendency make mine a bit thicker and add a touch of water at a time to get it to thin out to my desired consistency. Over the last few years I have found that in my attempts to be healthier I gravitate to using white meat for my fricassee. The flavor is different but it is still good. However, I ALWAYS use bone in meat and a combo of breasts AND Wings because of the flavoring that comes from bone in meat.

1 cut up chicken
½ pint of roux
2 quarts water
1 large onion
1 large green bell pepper
4 cloves of garlic
1 bunch onion tops/green onions
1 bunch parsley

Cut up raw chicken; season with salt and pepper. Boil water, add roux. Cook on medium-high heat for 20-30 minutes stirring until roux is completely dissolved. Add seasoned chicken, chopped onions, bell pepper, and garlic; return to a boil then reduce to low-medium heat for 30 minutes. Add parsley and onion tops; cook for 15 minutes. Cover to absorb all flavors and simmer until ready to serve. Serve the dish over white rice.

Your Ideas

Slow-cooker Chicken and Wild Rice

4 boneless, skinless chicken breasts
2 cups of chopped onion
1 (10.75 ounce) can of cream of mushroom soup
1 (6 ounce) package of long grain and wild rice with seasonings such as
 Uncle Ben's®, cooked according to package directions
2 cups chopped broccoli
1/2 teaspoon salt
1/2 teaspoon ground black pepper

Place chicken in a 4 quart slow cooker. Top with onion and soup. Cover and cook on low for 7 to 8 hours.

Before serving stir in cooked rice, broccoli, salt and pepper. Cook until heated through. Serve hot.

Note: Rice can be made the night before and stored in the refrigerator. Let cold rice cook for an additional 10 minutes after adding it to the slow cooker or until rice is heated thoroughly.

Mock Shu Corn

Nothing signals summer to me more than Mock Shu Corn. Maw was the best at this. Sitting on the carport with boxes and boxes of fresh picked summer corn meant that maw was gonna do some cooking and freezing of this fresh summer delight. My job was always the same. I would shuck the corn. Shucking was a job that my hyperactive behavior was perfect for. I could rip a hush off an ear of corn in no time flat. What would kill me was picking off all of that corn silk. Now that would drive any kid crazy! Maw would stand there with a big knife cutting cob after cob after cob of some of the juiciest corn I have ever seen. Big worn, silver aluminum tubs would be full and she would then start cutting green peppers and onions and garlic to add to the mixture and making her scrumptious mock shu. It was a very rare occasion that we would leave Maw's on a Sunday without a few backs of mock shu, and few bags of green beans, a jar or two of figs and or pears and sometimes even fish, shrimp, or sausage to tie us over until we made the trip back 3 or four weeks later. Maw and paw were two of the most generous people I have ever known. All of my aunts and uncles are still this way. Uncle Bud though makes me smile from ear to ear these days because you cannot even think about getting into the car empty handed. He is always saying here are some filets I cleaned for you or go pick some oranges grapefruit or kumkuats, or hey take this home and try it. It is just special. Now when he knows I am coming for a visit he will even go and buy or pick things to give to me the minute I arrive. Can you say warm cracklins??? But now back to the corn. Uncle Bud and Aunt Judy make a mean mock shu. I look forward to seeing them and hearing him tell me he has a bag of it in the freezer for me.

This dish does freeze quite well. Place in a freezer bag with the air removed. When you prepare this fresh, it is a very vibrant and colorful dish. I used a colored bowl to serve it in as it just adds a bit more zip and color! Enjoy!

8 ears of fresh corn
1 green bell pepper
1 purple onion
1 red bell pepper
3 tablespoons of butter
1/3 cup of water
Salt and pepper to taste

Shuck the corn and wash well. Dice bell peppers and onions. Take a good knife and cut the corn from the cob and set aside in a bowl. Once corn is removed from the cob, take the blade scrape down the length of the cobs to be sure to get all of the "corn and juice from the cob and remaining kernels. In a large sauté pan over medium heat, melt butter, add the water and sauté diced onions for about 3 to 5 minutes. Pour all cut corn and juice into pan and sauté for 5 minutes. Finally, add the bell peppers and continue to sauté for an additional 3 to five minutes. When done pour in a colorful serving owl and share with your family and friends.

HINT – If you are a fan of trying new things, peel 2 medium tomatoes, dice them up, sauté them with the onions and then add other ingredients that follow. Try other flavors if ya like and let me know how they go.

Cajun Crab Cakes

Now here is a recipe that I can give about 40 variations of. It seems as if as many people who love crab cakes have their own recipe for them. Herein lies the fun and fancy of making crab cakes. If you love a certain seasoning such as onion, garlic or crushed red pepper or even a little more different like blue cheese or spicy grain mustard, you can make it work with a basic crab cake. Over the years I have eaten more than my fair share of crab cakes – Let's just say I have eaten a Whole Heap of them…. I have found that the reason I love them so much is the CRAB!!! So when preparing my crab cakes, be prepared for more crab and less bread. I hope you enjoy these and even more so I hope you are sure to let me know what amazing varieties you have been able to create!

1 medium finely chopped red bell pepper (more or less a ½ cup)
1 medium finely chopped green bell pepper (about a ½ cup + or -)
4 whole sliced green onions
3 ½ teaspoons olive oil
2 or 3 cloves of garlic chopped
½ cup mayonnaise
1/3 cup chopped fresh parsley
2 large eggs slightly beaten
2 teaspoons Louisiana Hot Sauce
½ teaspoon dry old bay seasoning
2 teaspoons lemon zest
2 pounds fresh lump crabmeat
Olive oil Pam®
2 cups of crumbled cornbread OR bread crumbs

Sauté onions and peppers in olive oil for about 2 minutes and then throw in chopped garlic and sauté for 1 minute more. Remove from heat and set aside to cool for about 20 minutes. Next fold in mayo, eggs and seasonings and finally add crabmeat and choice of bread. I measure between 1/3 and ½ cup of the mixture and make into my patties and place them on a chilled pan and then cover tightly with plastic wrap and chill for about an hour to an hour and a half so that they will hold their shape.

Remove cakes from refrigerator and spray each side with olive oil Pam® and then in a large nonstick sauté pan on medium heat, cook each cake for about 4 to 4 and a half minutes or until they are nicely browned.

Serve with an amazing salad or with a flaky piece of grilled fish or a great grilled filet.

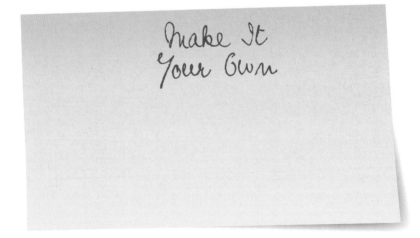

make It
Your Own

Cranberry Cravings

Kevin's Cranberry Relish

> 2 cups of fresh whole cranberries
> 1 small onion
> ¾ cup sour cream
> ½ cup sugar
> 2 tablespoons of red horseradish (in jar)

In a food processor, chunk cranberries and onion. Do not puree this!
Fold in sour cream sugar and horseradish. Refrigerate overnight.

This recipe is sure to add the most amazing shockingly bright color to your plate!
I love this served with very rich pork tenderloin as it cuts the richness and it adds
color like nobody's business. Kevin was right on with this one! Imagine that, my
brother recommends a bright colorful dish...

Cranberry Salad

> 2 small packs raspberry Jell-O®
> 1 ½ cups boiling water
> 1 can jellied cranberry sauce
> 1 cup chopped pecans
> 1 #2 can crushed pineapple
> 3 oranges chopped finely

Mix Jell-O® and hot water till dissolved. Add other ingredients stir and pour into
mold or dish you wish to serve in and refrigerate overnight.

Crabmeat Au Gratin

There is amazing flavor with this one! I could eat this every day – I would be 400 pounds but wow it has both crab and cheese. I can remember watching Mom make this and I was in complete amazement. She was creating this incredible smell. This looked like a magical dish to me, I even remember the bowls she placed the concoction in. She turned the light in the oven on and I watched the mixture bubble in the containers. By the time Mom pulled these blazing hot dishes out of the oven I had been sitting at the table napkin on my lap and practically drooling. It was complete torture for me to have to listen to mom tell me I had to wait another 5 minutes before I could eat. Of course, I offered to taste it to make sure it was ok and mom just looked at me and smiled. These days when I am home Mom often hits me on the shoulder with a spoon she has pulled out and says, "Go ahead and taste. Tell me if it needs anything and I will decide if it does or not." The smile is the same one I remember from when I was a little boy. Man, food is a very special thing!

A quick note to start with on this one....DO NOT USE IMITATION CRAB...

- 1 Cup Béchamel sauce – See recipe below
- 2 cups lump crabmeat
- 3 tablespoons of grated Romano cheese
- 3 tablespoons of grated Mozzarella cheese
- 3 tablespoons grated Swiss cheese
- ¼ cup breadcrumbs
- Salt and ground white pepper to taste

Mix Béchamel sauce and crabmeat. Add salt and pepper to taste and heat over medium heat for 1 minute.

Spoon the mixture into 6 small oven safe dishes. Combine cheeses and bread crumbs and sprinkle over tops. Bake in preheated oven on 375° until tops begin to brown. Remove and carefully serve.

Béchamel Sauce

- 2 tablespoons butter
- 2 tablespoons flour
- 1 ½ cup warm scalded milk
- Salt and ground white pepper to taste

Melt butter and stir in flour stir and cook without covering until mixture becomes foamy. Stir in the milk and bring to a boil, turn fire all of the way down to simmer on a gas stove on electric place on different burner that you have preheated to simmer. Add salt and pepper to taste. Remove from stovetop and dot the top with butter to prevent film from forming on the top.

Crawfish

My Uncle Pat was amazing. It seemed as if everything he ever touched turned to gold. In many ways, he was a mentor. Hell he was my godfather. He was an awesome mix of bayou and business and was always starting something new. One of his many ventures was crawfish. As a child, I didn't care for crawfish as something to be eaten. They were an object, when alive, that were meant to be played with and watched like you would a pet. To Uncle Pat, they were gold. He had crawfish ponds and took me out on those very cold damp Louisiana mornings to sit in a boat with him and watch him pull up cage after cage filled with the red treasures. I can remember going from trap to trap freezing and wet. Yet every time a trap came up out of the flooded rice field, I would laugh at the haul. Uncle Pat would just look back and laugh. In addition to farming them, Uncle Pat opened a successful crawfish processing plant. I was fascinated. Since he did many things well and taught me how to eat many different foods, I often times think my spirit of adventure and my willingness to try new things in my life are due to his courage and to his passion for life. I never get down about his passing but I do get inspired by him. I know I am a better person because of him and I know my cousin Chris and her husband Mike get their amazing work ethic from him as well. I hope a story of a man who inspires me to take risks and inspires me to love all of those around me makes you braver and makes you want to dig into life a bit more.

Crawfish Fettuccini

3 Vidalia onions (or yellow if can't get the Vidalia) chopped
3 ribs celery chopped
2 green peppers chopped
3 sticks butter
¼ cup flour
4 tablespoons parsley chopped
3 cloves garlic (or 4 if you are me) chopped
1 pint half and half
3 pounds crawfish tails
1 pound Velveeta® cheese
1 pound fettuccini noodles
Parmesan cheese
Salt and white pepper to taste

Sauté onions peppers and celery with the butter. Add flour cover and cook on low for 15 minutes stirring often. Add parsley and crawfish and cook for 15 minutes stirring often. Add half and half SLOWLY along with half of Velveeta® cheese. Add salt and pepper to taste and cook additional 30 minutes.
Add cooked noodles and place in casserole dish sprayed with Pam®. Top with parmesan cheese and remaining Velveeta®. Bake at 350° for additional 15 minutes or so.

Crawfish Etufette

5 pounds crawfish tails
1 cup of flour
1/3 cup vegetable oil
2 medium onions chopped
1 large green bell pepper chopped
2 (or if you are me 4 cloves garlic) chopped
Green onions and parsley to taste
1 small can tomato paste

Combine flour and oil and cook over low to medium heat stirring constantly until peanut butter brown add everything else except crawfish and green onion sauté till soft and then add crawfish and cook 10 to 15 minutes on low fire.

Serve over rice.

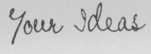

Your Ideas

Crawfish Jambalaya

As I shared earlier, it was Uncle Pat who really got me to love crawfish and this was one of his many recipes. . Many would consider this a 'cheat' recipe since it is not jambalaya in the traditional sense. Well good for you if you think that. I simply think back and remember an incredible meal with an uncle I loved.

This recipe is made in a rice cooker so first and foremost you need a rice cooker. A rice cooker is a pretty standard and humorous addition to any and all households in my family. When your roots are southwestern Louisiana and there are towns with rice festivals and rice queens and princesses, it is only natural that everyone has a good old rice cooker. I can still see Maw's big green Hitachi rice cooker steaming away on the counter. Nanny tends to give every niece and nephew a rice cooker for their wedding present. A basic rice cooker has an unattached lid with two settings, cook and warm. A rice cooker is nothing fancy or pressurized. It's a staple for any and all kitchens. One of the many things I Love about my family.

1 standard size can of beef broth (10 ½ oz)
1 onion chopped
1 green bell pepper chopped
1 Jalapeno pepper seeded and chopped
4 ounces of mushrooms chopped (if using jar or can drain rinse and chop)
1 stick of melted butter
1 pound of crawfish tails
2 ½ cups raw uncooked rice
1 8 ounce can of tomato sauce

Wash white rice and drain. Place all ingredients in rice cooker, stir and do not add water. Add a bit of salt and a dash or two of Louisiana Hot sauce and close up rice cooker. Turn rice cooker on to cook cycle. Once it has run the cycle do not open and leave on warm cycle for additional 30 to 45 minutes.

Hint: Do not double this recipe as it does not cook well.

Crawfish Noodles

2 tablespoons butter
1 onion (of your choosing) chopped
2 teaspoons of Dijon mustard
2 tablespoons of flour
2 pounds of crawfish tails
1 can of chicken stock
3 green onions chopped
Salt and pepper to taste
Louisiana Hot Sauce to taste
A handful of chopped parsley

Sauté onions in the butter until they are clear. Add the next 3 ingredients stirring constantly; slowly add the chicken stock until it makes a nice sauce. Add the seasoning and green onions and throw in parsley. Serve over cooked noodles.

You can add garlic – no big surprise here OR you can use a few drops of liquid crab boil instead of hot sauce. Be creative!

Crawfish and Shrimp Pasta

This is my fast and furious go to for a quick dinner. When I know I am going to be working late and want a good and filling meal, this is it. Everyone from Louisiana, look away now, I have even used frozen cooked shrimp for this one. I also mix it up a bit based on what flavor I'm craving.

3 cans of cream of shrimp soup
1 bunch of green onions
8 ounces rough chopped mushrooms
4 tablespoons butter
3 cloves of garlic or 4 or 5 LOL
1 teaspoon Louisiana Hot Sauce
2 pounds of crawfish tails
2 pounds of medium shrimp tails parboiled
1 pound cooked fettuccini
Parmesan cheese to taste (about ¼ cup)
Romano cheese to taste (about ¼ cup)

Sauté white ends of onions and mushrooms with butter and garlic for about 10 minutes, pour in soup and let simmer for an additional 7 to 10 minutes. Add hot sauce, salt and pepper to taste and add crawfish and simmer for 15 minutes... serve over cooked pasta and garnish with chopped green end of onions.

Green Bean Casserole

OK there is no secret weapon here. By now I would assume that more than half of the people in the U.S. have at least had this once. I would be insane to leave such a Thanksgiving staple out of this book. This super simple and yet classic dish is a part of so many great home-cooked meals. There are a few ways to spin this recipe that we will talk about online.

4 cans of French style green beans drained
2 and ½ cans of cream of mushroom soup
1 teaspoon of salt
1 teaspoon of coarsely ground black pepper
1 can of fried onions – I ALWAYS use the French's® brand

Mix all ingredients except for onions and pour into casserole dish. Bake on 350 for 35 minutes top with onions and then place back in onion for 15 more minutes. Serve!

Creamy Waldorf Salad

OK honesty time. As a child, this was never a favorite of mine. However the older I get, the more I find myself making this refreshingly yummy dish. It is the perfect side to a BLT, a chicken salad sandwich or even a grilled pork chop. This has always been a favorite of mom's and I know that it is always a hit when she brings it out.

4 ounces of cream cheese softened
1 ½ teaspoon of orange or pineapple juice
1 8 ounce can of pineapple tidbits drained
2 tablespoons of pecans chopped

1 ½ teaspoon sugar
3 large apples cubed
2 tablespoons celery chopped
2 tablespoons raisins

Combine cream cheese sugar and juice in a small bowl after you have let the cream cheese soften. Set aside.

Combine the remaining ingredients in a medium bowl add the cream cheese mixture and toss. Chill in the refrigerator and toss again before serving.

Dump Salad

Now here is the name of a dish that just makes you think, Ewwwww!!! I have got to admit I make this quite frequently and every time I make this dish I giggle and think of my mom. Mom has always been a woman who takes care of herself. She is an avid walker. Growing up I can remember a multitude of fad diets and ways of staying fit and or losing weight. This was a recipe a friend or neighbor gave her. I can remember her making this for the first time. I was disgusted by the name of the dish but could not help to be fascinated. I clearly remember laughing when she prepared the recipe since we finally got the joke about the name. This is low cal and low fat. I have this for breakfast or even for dessert and quite often as a little snack. It is quick, easy and actually pretty good. I have even used this as a layer in lighter healthier desserts.

1 24 ounce low fat cottage cheese
1 large can drained crushed pineapple in juice
1 12 ounce low fat cool whip thawed
1 6 ounce sugar free strawberry Jell-O®

Mix all together and place in refrigerator for a few hours and serve.

Oven Baked BBQ Baby Back Ribs

1 slab of baby back ribs
¼ cup Tony Chacherie's
¼ cup yellow mustard
¼ cup red wine vinegar
2 teaspoon Louisiana Hot Sauce

Carefully remove membrane on slab of ribs. Sprinkle all the above ingredients and rub over slab of ribs. Cover and place in refrigerator and marinate for at least 4 hours. I recommend marinating overnight.
Place in baking pan and seal tightly with aluminum foil. Place in oven on 250 for 6 hours basting at least once an hour with Sweet Baby Ray's or your favorite BBQ sauce.
The ribs will just fall apart and you will love every tender juicy bite. You've just made another amazing dish....keep up the good work!

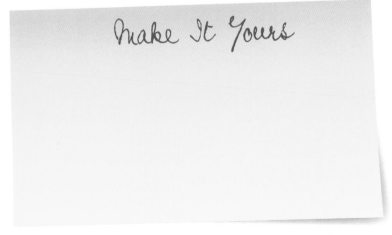

make It Yours

Dawn's Enchiladas (Chicken or Beef)

Dawn is my amazing step sister but a true sister all the same. In other words, she is not the animated movie kind of stepsister; you know the ones with crazy warts who are mean as all hell. She is sweet , kind, loving and an awesome addition to the family. The sad part is I hardly ever get to see her since she lives in Spokane, Washington and I am here in sunny Fort Lauderdale. It often seems as if we are worlds apart . The best part has been that we have both made an effort to stay in touch more and the few times I have made this recipe I always feel the need to call her and let her know how it went. So this is in the cookbook as a way to give my baby step sister a nod. Dawn I love you, I miss you and we have got to figure out how to see each other more often.

Now down to business. I have altered this almost every time I make it. I love to change up recipes. I have added one third to one half a pound of ground pork. I have added 2 chopped chipotle peppers to this. I have even topped this with mom's red beans! But you must know that I have ALWAYS doubled this recipe!

1 package enchilada sauce spices and seasoning – any brand will do look in the grocery aisle by the taco seasoning.

3 cups water

1 lb ground beef

1/3 cup chopped green bell pepper

2 cups shredded cheddar cheese (about 8 oz)

1 can (6 oz) tomato paste

1/3 cup chopped onion

8 corn tortillas

(If you are having more than 4 people, without a doubt double the recipe)

In a small bowl, mix water and tomato paste together with a fork. Next pour mixture into a saucepan, bring spices and seasonings, water and tomato paste to a boil.

Reduce heat to low and simmer uncovered, stirring occasionally, 10 min.

Brown ground beef, onion and bell pepper. Depending on the type of ground beef you are using I occasionally spoon off a bit of the grease. Stir in 1 cup cheese.

In 13X9 inch dish, pour 1 cup prepared sauce. Dip tortillas in remaining sauce, then evenly top with meat mixture. Roll up, then place seam side down in baking dish. Evenly top with remaining sauce.

Bake at 350 degrees for 15 minutes. Sprinkle with remaining 1 cup cheese and bake an additional 5 minutes or until cheese is melted.

Garnish top with 1/3 cup of finely chopped flat parsley, cilantro or green onion.

For Chicken Enchiladas - You can substitute 2 1/2 cups shredded cooked chicken for ground beef. I have used boneless skinless chicken breasts and to do so I use 4 tablespoons of olive oil and then the onion and bell pepper.

Whole Heap Hints – If you are like I often am, you will want to make this recipe over and over again. I have changed the flavors by adding green or black olives I use about a half of a cup chopped. I have added a peeled and seeded jalapeno.
I have also stirred in ½ of a small can of cream of mushroom soup to the beef after I have cooked it.

Maw's Green Beans

Now here is one for the books. You have already had the chance by now to read about my mornings with Maw. Maw was a hard worker but I do NOT want to neglect her other half. Paw was a workhorse. He always seemed like the largest man on the planet to me. I was never more fascinated by anything more than I was by his ability to grow just about anything. He grew garlic and onions, and tomatoes and cucumbers and beans, corn, figs, pears, watermelon, and and and......It never seemed to end. He could grow just about anything! He did it all including build the very house we slept in while we visited. I loved to sit in the swing next to him saying nothing and watching him drink his coffee and talk to me about what he needs. Though a very simple man by many standards, he was certainly the strong silent type. He was often a mystery to me but the one thing I have most certainly figured out about him was that he loved every single one of us, and most of all he loved Maw with every fiber of his being. Now here is a bit more about Maw. Maw used to make some of the best side food on the planet. I often think it was because we were lucky enough to have things fresh from the garden or from a local farmer. I can remember sitting on the car port with Maw snapping fresh beans. I have never again had some of the amazing dishes that maw used to make for weekend dinners. I often think it has to do with the memories. Maw's tired hands were riddled with arthritis yet she insisted on chopping, stirring, and pouring every bit of love in her 4'10" frame into every single thing she ever made for us. She was perfection in my eyes. The way she could love through her cooking never ceased to fill me with a sense of awe and at the same time make me want to be more like her in any and every way. She was the kindest soul I have ever met and the absolute definition of selflessness and love.

1/2 pound fresh green beans
1 can PET® milk
1/2 finely chopped medium onion
2 tablespoons butter

Snap ends off of green beans and break into bite sized pieces. Melt butter and sauté onions until translucent. On low/medium heat add pet milk and stir constantly. Bring to a low boil and after 3 minutes add green beans. Let green beans cook in mixture and allow milk to cook down and clot but not to scald. When done, serve with a slotted spoon and enjoy the country favorite of mine and think warm thoughts of family and home.

Grilled Country Style Pork Ribs

Now here is a recipe that makes me smile. Every single time that I grill I think about my family. Grilling pork is one of the things that makes me think of all of the men who were and are role models in my life. From Paw to Dad and Uncle Pat and Uncle Bud the sight of the smoke, the heat of the pit, the sound of laughter and stories, the smell of grilled meat and the incredible taste of the small bite of meat that I would sneak with Uncle Bud all make me love the grill even more. It was Uncle Bud and his "Cajun Microwave" or his freshly welded grill that always fascinated me. I have never had anything bad off of Uncle Bud's grill and I am always amazed at how dedicated to his craft of great grilling. Uncle Bud is another family treasure. He is hard-working and one of the most loving people you will ever meet. He wants those around him to know how tough he is but inside he is as soft and loving as ever. This recipe is different every single time I make it. It is always tender and delicious. Summer is always better when I can marinate a whole crock full of these ribs and then have a bunch of friends over and just start grilling. Remember I just mix, pour, shake and mix a bit more until I get the amount I need to marinate my meat in. Don't be scared. Be bold and adopt a method that will add a Whole Heap of flavor into whatever you want to grill and then share and enjoy.

Grilled Country Style Pork Ribs
(Continued)

4 pounds country style pork ribs
4 tablespoons yellow mustard
1 cup white vinegar
2 tablespoons Worestchire sauce
¼ teaspoon paprika
½ teaspoon of Louisiana Hot sauce
Fresh ground black pepper
Salt

In a bowl, mix all ingredients except ribs. After all are mixed well, dredge ribs through and place in a flat glass casserole pan. When done, pour remaining marinade over and refrigerate overnight. I have even let these sit for 2 days in the marinade.

About an hour or two before you are ready to grill the ribs remove from refrigerator and let come closer to room temperature. Heat grill to about 300 degrees and place ribs on grill and cook low and slow for about 30 to 45 minutes depending upon thickness of ribs.

Hints: I serve this with baked beans and roasted vegetables in the winter or mom's creamy potato salad or coleslaw in the summer. Make this your own and get to grilling. Always be careful about adding ingredients such as black pepper to this recipe as oftentimes it burns on the grill and leaves your meat tasting bitter.

Gumbo - Old School

As with any good southern Louisiana family, here is another recipe that is all about what you like. I have seen and tasted as many gumbos as there are restaurants in southern Louisiana. From dirty dishwater to thick as roux pastes, gumbo, for me, should be somewhere in the "brown water' category. Gumbo is meant to be served in a bowl with rice somewhere in the soup category rather than the rice and gravy category. Now are you confused? If you are, don't be. Gumbo is about love and the secret is in the roux and the chicken. Some people swear by okra and others hate it. Look to this recipe as your "tried and true" way of saying "hey I can't screw this one up." I look back onto many family gatherings in Rayne and chicken and sausage gumbo was the perfect complement to the gathering. From long weekends of damp cold to Christmas Eve gatherings with the family, a good gumbo is a gathering meal. You can put a big pot of gumbo on and still visit with friends and family while you make your house warm and welcoming. From holidays to cold winter football Saturdays and Sundays, gumbo is THE way to go. One of my most recent and wonderful memories happened ever so recently. Mom came to Florida to help with the cookbook and we got to hang out, celebrate Jeff's birthday and make a mean pot of gumbo. The best part of the story is that mom managed to bring the sausage all of the way from Louisiana to beautiful South Florida. Now get busy and get cooking this fantastic family favorite!

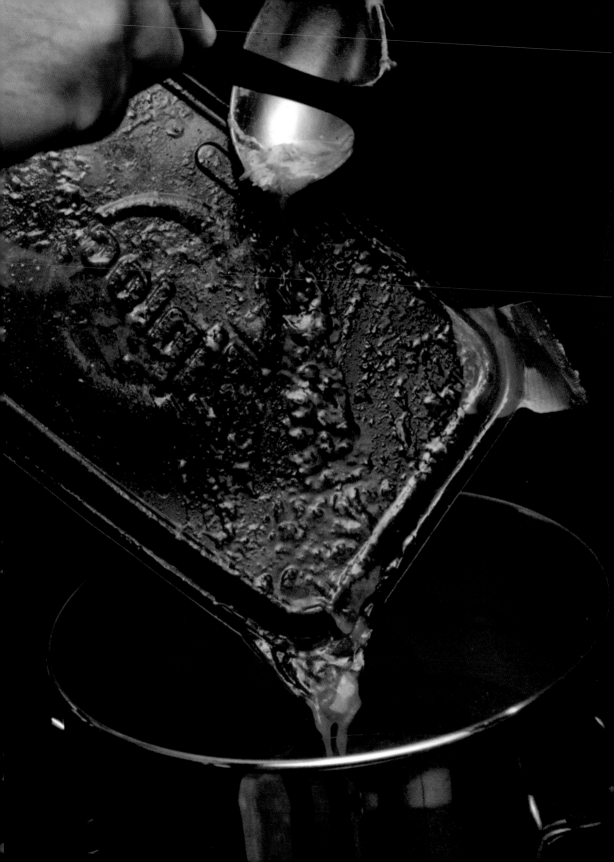

1 whole chicken cut up – an extra couple of breasts or thighs if you like
1 1/2 pounds of smoked sausage
2 medium onions chopped
2 medium green bell peppers chopped
10 cloves of garlic chopped
2 bunches of green onion
2 large bunches of parsley chopped
1/2 cup of roux
96 ounces of water

Brown chicken in 2 1/2 tablespoons of cooking oil in the bottom of your stock pot. The goal here is to give the chicken some good color and to release the juices. Once chicken is browned add water, onions, bell pepper and garlic and bring to a boil. Once stock is boiling, add roux and dissolve. Once roux has dissolved you should have a good brown color to your stock. Boil for 30 minutes and then add parsley and green onion. Boil for next 20 minutes then add sausage to mixture and simmer for 20 minutes more. During the simmering time I often remove each piece of chicken, debone it, throw out the bones, and put the chicken back into the stock. This just makes it easier to eat for your family and friends.

I always serve this with Maw's bread and butter pickles and either a good baked sweet potato OR Mom's creamy potato salad!!!

Seafood Gumbo

I have been asked time and time again why I put gumbo in the entrée section of the cookbook rather than the soup section. The best answer that makes the most sense to me is that I did it because I wanted to. I know this sounds crazy, but I have always seen gumbos as meals and not as something one has before the meal. In any sense, it is why I did it and it is yet another reason why this is not your typical or ordinary cookbook. Let's remember I never set out to write a cookbook. I set out to tell you a story of what it is like to have grown up as me.

- 2 medium onions
- 2 medium green bell peppers
- 4 cloves garlic
- 1 bunch green onion tops
- 1 bunch parsley
- 3 pounds medium shrimp peeled and de-veined
- 1pound crab meat
- 10 cups water
- 10 oz. roux

Boil water and roux stirring 15 to 20 minutes to ensure roux is completely dissolved. Add chopped onions, bell peppers, and garlic; bring to a boil and then turn heat down to low-medium. Add shrimp, onion tops and parsley for 15 minutes. Add crab meat and cook about 5 minutes on low. Turn off heat, cover and let sit to absorb all flavors.

Grilled Grouper

Now this is a southern summer favorite of mine and baby is it ever easy! I most recently made this for mom and Jeff while they were here for a visit and we had the most amazing time during this meal. We have all been trying to watch our weight as well as trying to get a bit more fit. This recipe fits the bill as far as we were concerned. The following recipe is for 2 people. Feel free to add as many grouper fillets as you like.

2 8 ounce fillets of grouper
1 lime
1 teaspoon salt
1 teaspoon ground black pepper
¾ teaspoon Ground red pepper
Olive oil

Pour olive oil in plate and place fillet into the oil then flip. Repeat with second fillet. Mix dry ingredients and then sprinkle on both sides of fillets and place on pan. Cut lime in half and squeeze half onto fillets. Let sit for 5 minutes. Place fillets onto low grill (about 350 degrees) placing the lime side down. Squeeze lime onto other side while on grill. Let fish cook for 6 minutes. Flip fillets and grill for remaining 5 minutes watching closely. Remove and serve... Simple healthy and delicious!!!! I love this with roasted asparagus as well as my roasted summer vegetable medley!

Macaroni and Cheese

You know it is rare to have someone come along in life who you can truly connect with in so many ways with so many things and yet be so totally different. Mom and Miss Diane were just that.

1 8 ounce package large elbow macaroni cooked
1 tablespoon olive oil
1 cup mild cheddar cheese
2 cups sharp cheddar cheese shredded
1 12 ounce can evaporated milk
4 ounces half and half
3 eggs beaten
Salt and pepper to taste
Butter large baking dish

Pour 1 layer of cooked macaroni into baking dish. Add salt and pepper over the top. Add a layer of the cheeses. Add layer of macaroni and add last of cheese.

Beat eggs and milk together. Pour mixture over macaroni. Bake on 350° for 30 to 40 minutes uncovered. Do NOT over bake.

HINTS – 1/2 stick butter can be added to this for and extra rich flavor but I often skip it. It is OK to remove this from the oven if it is still a little soupy. It will set after 5 minutes or so and will still be very hot for serving.

The other fun thing to do is get creative with this dish....Try using goat cheese or blue cheese or pepper jack to add a whole heap of a spin to this favorite classic.

Jeff's Heavenly Grilled Ham

Jeff is my stepdad. Having met, dated and married my mom years after dad passed, Jeff has become an incredible part of our lives. He has become very important to me and I love him so very much. Jeff is helpful in the kitchen and made his mark with mom's side of the family when he made this ham for his first big Cajun family Christmas. The year he volunteered to make the ham, Mom, of course, called the family and asked. There was a bit of hesitation but Jeff was allowed to make the ham. We brought the ham and, no surprise to me, there was a second ham there... just in case. The funny part was Jeff's ham was a hit. Every bite of it was gone while the other ham sat there and just looked sad and uneaten. Well needless to say, Jeff now makes the ham every year for Christmas and we all love what he brings to the favorite of family holidays.

8 to 10 pound ham (with or without bone)
16 to 18 ounces of Bourbon Whiskey – I also pour an additional 2 ounces over ice and add a splash of ginger ale, for some reason I LOVE the way everything ends up tasting!!!
1/2 cup brown sugar
1/2 teaspoon garlic salt
1/2 teaspoon cloves
1/2 teaspoon Louisiana Hot Sauce
1/4 teaspoon curry salt
1 teaspoon cinnamon
1 teaspoon finely chopped garlic
1 cup crushed pineapple with juice

Mix all ingredients in large bowl. Cut 2 parallel 2 to 3 inch cuts in the top of the ham to allow the juices to soak in. Place ham in a disposable aluminum deep baking pan and baste with the mixture. Spoon out the pineapple and place it over the slits in the ham.

Place the ham and pan onto a BBQ grill on medium heat. Keep liquid in a bowl and with a brush baste the ham every 15 minutes and keep the BBQ grill closed. Your ham should be done in 90 to 100 minutes.

Keep a touch of liquid in the bottom of the pan to keep your ham extra moist. This is an awesome holiday meal that you can prepare with relative ease.

Once you have let your ham cool, go ahead and slice it and enjoy some of the best ham of your life! If you want to, save some larger chunks from the outside of your ham and set it aside you will have some amazing seasoning for amazing black eyes or even a good slow cooked pot of red beans.

Make It Yours

Lasagna

I always knew when our annual summer vacation was really close because the weekend before we left, mom would almost always make a lasagna. To this day, when I make her lasagna I feel as if I am getting ready for a vacation. The Saturday or Sunday before we would be leaving New Orleans for our annual family vacation mom made this lasagna. Each and every year for as far back as I can remember we would pack up the car and hit the road bound for Destin Florida where would stay at Jetty East. Our usual condo that we rented was 112-A or 112-B. Yes there are photos from the time mom was pregnant all of the way up to the time mom, Kevin, and I went after dad had passed. There was nothing fancy about our family vacations; just the four of us coming together and spending a week away from home and with each other. From sunrises to sunsets, Jetty East in Destin had this magic about it which included Mom's lasagna.

This is a large recipe so it is not one for you to make for just yourself and 1 guest, unless he/she eats like a champion (the way I do) or you are planning to freeze it in pieces. Otherwise, I would strongly suggest making this for your family or having a few people over to share this magical, meaty, molten dish.

Make It Yours

5 pounds of ground meat
3 yellow onions
3 green bell peppers
13 cloves of garlic
1 can of tomato paste
1 can tomato sauce
1 cup of red wine
2 containers of cottage cheese
2 pounds mozzarella cheese
1 1/2 pounds Swiss cheese
Usually about a box and a half of lasagna noodles

Brown ground meat onions peppers and garlic until there is no juice left. Add tomato paste and stir for about 3 to 4 minutes. Add tomato sauce and red wine and simmer for 1 hour to 1 1/4 hours.

Cook noodles according to directions on box and let cool.

Shred cheeses while sauce is simmering. Layer noodles, then meat, then cottage cheese, then grated cheese. Repeat layers until pan is full and to with final layer of shredded cheese. Bake at 325° for 1 hour.

Let lasagna rest for 5 minutes before slicing and serving.

Momma's Creamy Potato Salad

This is a great recipe for family BBQ's or a night when you want to have people over for a big pot of Gumbo or even a great gathering where some good old Southern comfort flavor should come into play. Nothing says summer BBQ to me the way a heaping serving of this chilled treat does. Many times I will make this recipe and pick on the leftovers for the rest of the week. It makes a good bit but once again feel free to make it your own and alter it to make it Wholly Special for you and your friends and family.

5 pounds of red potatoes
1 dozen eggs
1 medium onion finely chopped
1 small red pepper chopped
3 stalks of celery chopped
4 or 5 dill pickles chopped
1 cup of mayonnaise – you may use more if you want it creamier up to another 1/2 cup
1/3 cup yellow mustard – again feel free to use more if you want a little more color

Cut up and oil potatoes until tender. Boil eggs separate from the potatoes. Peel and finely chop your eggs. Drain your potatoes and mix all ingredients together until creamy and you have your desired consistency and color. Add salt and pepper to taste. This can be served hot or cold and it is simply delicious either way!

Hints - I often garnish with chopped fresh parsley and fresh cracked black pepper. If you want to add a bit of zing add 1 or 2 tablespoons of Louisiana Hot Sauce to the potatoes when boiling them and then garnish with crushed red pepper flakes. I also make this dish the night before and leave in the refrigerator overnight to make sure it is fully chilled when I serve it at BBQ's.

Make It Yours

Oven Baked Potato Wedges

2 large white potatoes
2 sweet potatoes – or as I grew up knowing them...YAMS
2 tablespoons olive oil
1 tablespoon Parmesan
1 teaspoon paprika
3/4 teaspoon garlic salt
1/2 teaspoon thyme
1/4 teaspoon black pepper

Cut potatoes lengthwise into approximately 8 wedges. Arrange on an ungreased pan skin side down. Mix remaining ingredients together and brush onto the potatoes and bake at 375° for 45 to 50 minutes.

Make It Yours

Meat Balls and Spaghetti

Meatballs

2 lbs. ground sirloin	6 cloves garlic
1 bunch fresh parsley	I bunch???? tops
1 tablespoon Tony Chachere's	1/3 cup seasoned bread crumbs
1/3 cup Parmesan cheese	1/4 cup milk
2 eggs beaten	1/2 cup vegetable or olive oil

Chop all seasonings. Add meat, eggs, cheese, milk and bread crumbs. Form meatballs. Fry in oil. Remove and begin to prepare sauce.

Sauce

2 medium onions	6 cloves chopped garlic
1 green bell pepper	2 stalks celery
1/4 cup olive oil	1 bunch parsley
4 whole bay leaves	2 large jars of prepared spaghetti sauce

Chop seasonings. Heat oil in heavy pot; add seasonings. Cook for 10-15 minutes on medium heat. Add 2 jars of prepared sauce, bay leaves and parsley. Simmer for 15 minutes then add meatballs. Reduce heat to low and cook for 1/2 hour or until you are satisfies with thickness. Serve over spaghetti and top with freshly grated Parmesan cheese.

Slow Cooker Pulled Pork

Here is one for the books. I mean really... who doesn't like a good pulled pork? A sumptuous, Southern favorite, pulled pork's biggest secret is cooking it low and slow. In other words cook this in a slow cooker or crock pot and keep the temperature LOW. This is one of those recipes that makes me want to have people over. It is a meal that can truly be enjoyed and everyone loves the ability to mix and mingle with guests and still be able to serve a Southern favorite. Now as far as your sauce is concerned, those in the Carolinas or in Texas or in the Midwest all have their favorites and that is just fine with me. Use whatever sauce you prefer. But here I am going to give you a few of my slow cooker pulled pork secrets and you then decide what sauce to soak your biscuit in.

I ALWAYS use a larger pork tenderloin than I think I will need because I LOVE pulled pork leftovers. Trust me, so will your friends and family so go a bit overboard with the size of your pork loin.

> 4 pounds of pork tenderloin
> 4 tablespoons of Worsterchire® sauce
> 4 tablespoons yellow mustard
> 4 ounces of Bourbon!!! And 1 or two
> more ounces for yourself!!!
> 1 finely chopped onion
> 5 cloves of garlic finely chopped
> 1/2 teaspoon paprika
> 1 teaspoon freshly ground black pepper
> 1/2 teaspoon ground white pepper
> 4 teaspoons honey

Mix all ingredients except pork in a bowl with a wire whisk. Leave pork loin in as large of pieces as possible. I usually cut mind in half. Sprinkle Tony Chachere's original Creole seasoning all over the pork loin. Let loin sit for an hour or so in the refrigerator. After letting pork rest with the seasoning, place in large crock pot on high. Pour liquid over the top of pork loin and let cook for 1 hour. After first hour, lower temp to low and let cook for another hour. Then add 1 cup of BBQ sauce. This is where you can make this your own. Let pork cook for 2 to 2 ½ more hours. You know your pork is done when you stick a fork in it and it pulls apart (the old stick a fork in it and it's done).

Once your pork is ready take it out and place it on a chopping board and use two forks and pull it apart. Look at liquid in crock pot and if there seems to be too much grease, it will be sitting on top. Remove at least half of the grease. Do not remove all of the grease as you will need some of it in order to keep the pork from becoming dry. Shred down the pork loin into pieces and place back into crock pot and let it continue to cook on warm for another 30 minutes so the pork can soak up all of those wonderful juices.

Let pork continue to soak up for last 30 minutes. I LOVE to serve this dish in a unique way. I heap the pork and juice over one or two of maw's awesome country biscuits. If you want that true southern BBQ taste any time of year, serve over the biscuit AND add some of my Momma's creamy potato salad.

Oven-baked Pork Chops

Oh boy Oh Boy Oh Boy... The kitchen smells like home. I LOVE a good bone in pork chop. Mom has been making these delicious things in the oven for what seems to be my entire life. These do definitely differ from dad's amazing chops on the grill. I can see it now... pork chops, Maw's green beans and a baked yam or an amazing sweet potato casserole. These slow cooked chops will simmer and sputter and then just fall apart. Talk about an amazing post football Sunday dinner.

4 thick pork chops at least 1 _ inch thick
2 tablespoons yellow mustard
2 tablespoons Worcestershire® sauce
1 lemon
1/2 cup water
1 tablespoon Tony Chachere's seasoning

Season pork chops with all above ingredients except water and lemon. Squeeze lemon over chops. Cover and refrigerate for 2 hours. Add water just before placing in oven. Preheat to 350.

Place chops in oven, covered for 30 minutes then turn chops for another 30 minutes. Uncover and continue to cook for 15 minutes or until the color of the chops is nice and brown.

Heinen Bread Dressing

YYou have already heard e talk about Aunt Annie and Uncle Pat. Well Aunt Annie's family was aclose-knit German family from Robert's Cove, Louisiana. Aunt Annie was originally Heinen. The following recipe is from her family as passed down through the years and I know I have played with this recipe as well and I really enjoy it as it is one of the best basic dressing bases going. So sit back and enjoy a little more of southwest Louisiana with a bit of German flair.

7 or 8 lbs ground chuck
1 bunch celery-stalks chopped
3 large onions chopped
Bell peppers (1 green, 1 yellow & 1 red) chopped,
6 cloves garlic chopped (BUT let's face it I use 8 or 9)
6 or 7 eggs
Old French bread or buns or croutons (equivalent to 15-20 slices of bread)
Onion tops & parsley chopped
Season to taste

Soak bread in water – squeeze out water & place in bowl. Cook ground meat in a little oil (3 to 4 tablespoons). When brown add celery, peppers, onions & garlic. Cook until vegetables are soft. Add bread, eggs & season well (Tony Chachere's seasoning). It needs to stay moist so add broth when needed. Add onion tops & parsley. Place in large roasting pan & put in oven at 325 to 350 degrees until brown, adding broth as needed. About 2 hours. Add seasoning if needed.

Red Beans and Rice

It is very sad to admit but it was at the very end of this book and it's photography that Frank asked me "where are the red beans?" I reviewed the book over and over again only to notice that I have left out probably one of the most delicious and important staples of New Orleans cooking. I was appalled with myself. New Orleans is known for red beans on Mondays. The dish is a standard and is known for Mondays in New Orleans because Mondays were always laundry days and this is a dish that could be left o the stove for hours upon end without ruining it. This generations old tradition is still alive and well in many New Orleans restaurants who still serve red bens a a special on their menu on Mondays.

Red beans are varied in the way in which they are prepared and served, but for me the best part is the warmth they give the soul when you eat a good bowl of them, Consistency of red beans is often up to the one who prepares them. I prefer mine a bit thicker and richer. As a simple confession, I use bacon, ham and sausage in my red beans. I still use Mom's pot to make my beans and I still make more than I could possibly eat simply to have enough to put some in the freezer.

Step one is to pour beans into a large bowl and fill bowl with water. You must allow 3 to 4 inches of height for the beans to swell up and grow. I let my beans soak for at least a few hours and oftentimes let them soak over night.

In a large pan cook bacon until done and set aside. I SAVE the Grease!

Then, in a large pot use a couple of teaspoons of the bacon grease and sauté onion and bell pepper for about 5 minutes on medium heat. Add garlic and sauté for an additional minute. Pour 5 cups of water and add beans. Bring to a boil and then turn heat down to low and allow to simmer. Once heat has been turned down to low, add ham, cooked bacon and Tony Chacherie's. It is at this time that you should check to make sure the water in the post is about 2 inches over the top of your beans.

1 Pound of red kidney beans
1 large Onion chopped
1 large green bell pepper chopped
4 or 5 cloves of garlic
1 tablespoon Tony Chacherie's seasoning
1 pound of bacon
1 pound ham – I generally use the outer skin of the Heavenly Ham found in the book.

Stir beans well and allow to cook on low for the next 90 minutes stirring about every 25 to 30 minutes. I like to leave my pot covered. After 90 minutes, cut sausage up and add to mixture and allow to simmer for an additional 30 minutes.

If when you are through with your cook time you do not like the consistency of your beans take 2 cups place them in a bowl and mash them up and stir them back into the mixture.

When all is done take a large ladle and pour beans over cooked rice and serve.

HINT – I often make 2 pounds of beans at a time and make individual containers to freeze so dinner after a long day at the office can still be delicious and a perfect end to my day.

Rice Dressing

Another Thanksgiving and Christmas staple in my family. Nothing beats this one, except the cornbread dressing made with Maw's cornbread. Rice dressing is always the responsibility of either Aunt Net at Christmas and Mom's at Thanksgiving. Either way it is ALWAYS an absolute hit and something that I can eat till I feel a little dizzy. One of my favorite parts about making this is that I get to use my Mom's old Magdelite® roast pan. Just using the pan can bring me back to our old kitchen and I can remember the aromas coming from this special pot. It is something I will always treasure and it is part of what makes cooking this rice dressing a whole heap of special. The meat portion of the rice dressing can be prepared beforehand. It stores well in the refrigerator or freezer. I ALWAYS double this recipe because I love it so much and because of the fact that I just can't get enough of it. I am often surprised by how many people have never had or even heard of this dish and so it makes it even more fun to prepare for people. I just LOVE LOVE LOVE cooking this, most importantly, I LOVE eating this!

1 pound of ground beef	1 pound of ground pork
2 medium onions	2 medium green bell peppers
1 large bunch of parsley	1 can of cream of mushroom soup
1 large bunch of green onion	2 tablespoons of roux
2 tablespoons of Tony Chachere's	

1 whole head – not clove but the whole head – garlic chopped

On medium to high heat brown beef and pork and shake Tony Chachere's over while browning. It is important that you brown the meat in order to achieve that great color. After about ten minutes, add chopped onions, bell peppers and garlic and mix well. Once you notice the onions becoming translucent add parsley and green onions. Stir frequently for next 10 minutes.

Now add 3/4 cup of water and the roux stirring in order to dissolve the roux and mix the cream of mushroom soup fully. Once roux is dissolved and the cream of mushroom soup is mixed throughout, lower heat to medium/low and simmer for 30 minutes.

Once you have lowered the heat go ahead and cook 2 cups of uncooked rice. Once rice is ready, mix into meat _ cup at a time until you have desired consistency.

The other AMAZING option with this is to use maw's cornbread instead of rice and enjoy a delicious cornbread dressing and believe me that is one treat of a side dish.

This is excellent with BBQ pork, baked turkey, roasted chicken or heck even by itself. I hope you can enjoy this as much as I do.

MAW'S ROAST

From Maw to Mom to Me –
The roast that melts in your mouth!!!

For as long as I can remember I have been served this incredible meal. I went through a phase from age 5 to 8, where I refused to enjoy roast beef more out of stubbornness than anything else. Now I crave it.. The slower and longer you cook the roast the better it it tastes as it absorbs more of the flavors and seasoning. I always feel the love when I make this country basic. I feel home and heritage and know how proud Maw and Mom are of me. I can remember clear as a bell arriving at maw's in the evening and the whole house smelling of this awesome dish. I always knew I was home. This is one of those dishes that inspires me, and makes me feel the warmth of family like nothing else. From cold winter evenings to Sunday evening dinners this is a classic not to be topped. I now have friends who ask me to cook this one when I invite them over for dinner. For the full-on, Southern Louisiana taste, I prepare the roast with mock shue corn and Maw's green beans. All I need to do is write the names of these dishes down and my mouth begins to water and a sense of home envelopes me.

4 to 5 pound roast about 2.5 inches thick. – Season with salt and pepper and sprinkle with Louisiana Hot Sauce
1 large or 2 medium Vidalia onions
1 large or 2 medium green bell peppers
7 to 9 LARGE cloves of garlic – you know me and my love of garlic!
1 or 2 large packages of sliced mushrooms – optional but I Love em

In a Large roasting pan pour 6 to 8 tablespoons of olive oil and heat. Get oil and pan Very hot and then sear roast for about 3 minutes on each side. Remove roast and dump in chopped vegetables from above and allow them to brown stirring constantly with wooden spoon. To brown the seasonings will take about 7 to 9 minutes.

Add about 3 cups of water and allow to come back to a boil. Once boiling turn down to medium to low and put meat back in and allow to cook while covered for another hour to an hour and 15 minutes.

Hint – If you would like slightly thicker gravy you can add cornstarch or flour 1 teaspoon at a time.

Another great hint is once this is cooked place in a glass container and store until next day in the refrigerator and put back in pot and warm on LOW until heated all of the way through.

Roux

Roux equals magic. I was recently having a conversation with my dear friend Charlene. She and I were discussing this book and the magic of food and the ways in which we make it all come together. We talked about people's red beans and other people's ways of cooking their own special dish. Her exact words to me were, "Chad people need to realize that food changes, it evolves and it's never the same thing twice." Now for someone writing a cookbook, this is a frightening concept, however she is right. Everyone makes a different gumbo, pot of beans or fricassee. The same can be said of a good Southern roux. Roux is the heart of Gumbo and fricassee and I have been known to add it to several random dishes just because I happen to come across it in the fridge. Just as an FYI, I ALWAYS have roux on hand in my fridge. Roux can now be bought in the store and even comes in several powder forms. When my recipes call for roux, I am talking about home-made roux NOT the powder.

Roux is always made in my skillet. Over the last few years I make it in my enamel coated skillet. Making roux always brings me back to my childhood. I HATED the smell of it as a child BUT was always mesmerized with the magic that it created. Roux was always added to my favorite dishes so I just knew it had to be magical. I simply could not wrap my head around the fact that two simple ingredients could make something taste and become so darned delicious. Mom could not stand it when I wanted to be in the kitchen when she was making roux. I thought she was just giving me grief and saying she didn't want me to know what she was putting into it. So what I ended up learning after moving out of the house was that mom wanted me out because roux can bite ya back! WARNING: Roux BURNS!!! Roux's magic is HOT oil so be careful when preparing this and use a trusted wooden spoon for stirring.

You have got to pay attention when cooking this amazing ingredient. I always start with equal parts flour and cooking oil. The secret to good roux...keep stirring. Roux goes from perfect to burned pretty fast so remember as soon as your roux looks like dark peanut butter TURN off the stove. The heat of your cast iron will keep on cooking this and you don't want it to burn.

1 1/3 cups cooing oil
1 1/3 cups flour

After this cook at 1 minute intervals stirring well between each time until you have a rich peanut butter color.
I always remove my roux from the skillet and immediately get into an oven safe glass dish. Once roux is completely cooled I store mine in a ramekin or even an old mason jar. You can store your roux this way for up to 6 weeks.

Shrimp Kabobs with Rice

1 pound of large peeled shrimp
1 15 1/4 ounce can of pineapple chunks
1 8 ounce bottle of Italian dressing
1 8 ounce can tomato sauce
3 tablespoons brown sugar
1 1/2 teaspoons yellow mustard
1 medium green bell pepper cubed

Drain pineapple and save about 1/4 cup of the juice. Combine the saved juice, Italian dressing, tomato sauce, sugar and mustard in a dish. Add shrimp to mixture and toss gently to coat cover and place in refrigerator for at least 2 hours to marinate. Remove shrimp from marinade and save remainder for basting.

Place shrimp and peppers on skewers and grill 3 or 4 minutes and serve over rice. You can cook down marinade for 15 minutes over medium heat to have sauce to serve on rice and let's face it everything is better when covered in a delicious sauce.

Herbed Seared Tuna Steak

I must admit I was never a big fresh fish kind of guy until about 7 or 8 years ago. I was afraid of cooking fish. Over the last year, I have lost over 80 pounds and I must admit I have changed the way I eat. This is one of the dishes I have enjoyed eating and have enjoyed experimenting with. If you are not a fan of tarragon, use dill.

- 2 or 3 garlic cloves
- 2 teaspoons fresh tarragon
- 2 teaspoons fresh cilantro
- 4 teaspoons extra virgin olive oil
- 4 tablespoons lemon juice
- 1/2 teaspoon salt
- 1/2 teaspoon black pepper
- 2 8 ounce of tuna fillets raw. I enjoy blue fin and even a yellow fin
- 21 fresh asparagus spears
- 2 potatoes, medium baked

Prepare marinade. Finely chop garlic, tarragon and cilantro. Combine with oil, lemon juice, salt and pepper in a shallow non-reactive dish or plastic freezer bag. Marinate tuna for at least 30 minutes or as long as 2 hours. Remove tuna and set

Grill asparagus until tender and then remove from grill. Sear tuna on a very hot grill for 1-2 minutes on each side to desired doneness or temperature. Tuna dries out easily so take care not to overcook it.

Spinach and Artichoke Casserole

If you can imagine, this is a thicker version of spinach and artichoke dip. I don't think there is anything wrong with serving this as a side dish. This casserole is most certainly a recipe that can be altered to meet your desires. The bottom line.... most people love this type of dish so why not play with it and make it wholly yours. Be brave be bold and remember, Dig in!

12 ounces of cream cheese softened
1 jar marinated artichoke hearts chopped
1 10 ounce box frozen chopped spinach
3/4 cup mushrooms chopped
Parmesan cheese
Italian bread crumbs
Salt and black pepper to taste

Mix softened cream cheese and softened butter well. Add spinach and artichokes. Butter pan well or use liberal amount of Pam®. Dust the bottom and sides of the pan with breadcrumbs and Parmesan. Add the mixture and sprinkle the top again with the breadcrumbs and cheese and bake at 330° for 30 to 35 minutes.

Sweet Potato Casserole

A holiday favorite or let's face it an overall favorite comfort food of mine this amazing dish is sure to bring a smile to your face and put a bit of southern cheer into your stomach. This dish is quite easy and goes well with a roasted turkey, baked ham, or slow roasted pork chops. I often laugh at the number of people who say they do not like sweet potatoes yet they go back for serving after serving of this sweet and lovely dish.

3 large cans of sweet potatoes drained then mashed
1 cup of sugar
4 eggs beaten
1 teaspoon salt
1/2 cup butter melted
1 cup of milk
4 or 5 teaspoons of vanilla
Mix all well and drop into large glass baking dish

Topping

1 cup brown sugar firmly packed
2/3 cup flour
2/3 cup melted butter
2 cups chopped pecans

Mix sugar and flour together...Mix with remaining ingredients and spoon on top of casserole. Bake at 350° for 35 to 40 minutes. Now this was easy and OMG is this ever Delicious!!!!

OVEN ROASTED VEGETABLE MEDLEY

Now here is a recipe that I came up with as a result of my interesting relationship with my vegetarian yogi friend, Rebecca. I would say that our meeting was accidental, but she would say "No, no, no, we met because the universe put us together... and that it was our energy that pulled us together." Rebecca is one of the most supportive and reassuring people I have ever met. Her friendship has made me a better person. Her peace and balanced nature has helped me to be more confident, more loving and more passionate about life as a whole. I created this dish specifically for her, and I find myself preparing the dish more and more often even though I am a fierce meat eater. Surprisingly, even my meat-loving friends and family LOVE it.

This recipe is full of color and vibrant flavors. The vegetables are readily available and you can serve this side with any grilled protein.. I am a firm believer that the key to this fantastic dish is using the freshest vegetables you can find so subsititute with whatever is available.

Yet another twist for this dish.....make extra and refrigerate. The next day, add fresh stewed tomatoes or tomato paste to create a simply delicious pasta sauce that you and yours will enjoy for days to come.

2 large purple onions
1 Green Bell Pepper
1 yellow Bell pepper
1 Red bell pepper
2 green zuchinni
2 yellow squash
1 head of garlic peeled
1 package button mushrooms (I often experiment with different types of mushrooms)
4 medium stalks of fresh rosemary
1 tablespoon Italian seasoning
1/3 cup olive oil
Salt and pepper to your flavor preference

Preheat oven to 400 degrees. Cube all vegetables and mix the Italian seasoning and olive oil salt and pepper. Pour mixture over cubed vegetables and mix with hands. Put vegetables into roasting pan. Place rosemary springs in center of vegetables and place in oven cook for 20 minutes, remove stir and roast for last 25 minutes.

HINT: If you have leftovers...bake 4 tomatoes in oven, puree them and mix into the cooked vegetables and serve over pasta! This will be one sauce you are going to love.

Again, this recipe is the perfect side to go with grilled fish, steak, pork, or chicken. Cut onion and peppers, into 1 inch cubes. Peel cloves of garlic. Cut squash and zucchini long wise and then cut into ½ inch pieces. Toss all veggies with olive oil

and mix with remainder of ingredients. Rough chop basil leaves and mushrooms and toss all ingredients and throw into roasting pan.

Place pan in oven that has been preheated to 400 degrees and roast vegetables for 45 to 50 minutes . Mix up or stir veggies once about half way through time. Remove pan from oven and let veggies sit for 3 to 5 minutes before serving.

Hint – if you want to change up this flavor use 2 tablespoons of olive oil and 3 or 4 tablespoons of balsamic vinegar.

make It Yours

Desserts

Blueberry Pie

It doesn't get more basic than this recipe. Simple desserts rock and often are the best dishes. Enjoy this one!

2 cups of blueberries
½ cup sugar
½ cup chopped pecans
2 eggs
1 cup of sugar
1 cup flour
½ cup butter (melted)
½ cup shortening (melted)

Grease a 10" pie plate well with butter or Pam.

Pour blueberries into pie plate. Sprinkle ½ cup sugar and nuts over berries. Beat egg well and add 1 cup of sugar and beat thoroughly. Add flour, melted butter, and the shortening to the egg-sugar mixture. Beat well and pour over the top of the berries.

Bake at 325 for one hour. Don't forget to let it cool before serving!

MOM'S BEST AND EVERYONE'S FAVORITE BREAD PUDDING!!!

Now back up and LOOK OUT!!! This is a recipe that you can make your own in countless ways. The basics are all here for something truly amazing. I have had this simply fantastic dessert mixed up 50 different ways. .

We were never a huge sweets or dessert family. Now once you stop laughing and peel yourself up off of the floor, I want you to think about the following story. As a child I noticed that my Dad would do anything for bread. He could have it for breakfast, snack on a piece of croissant midday, have a sandwich on French bread for lunch, and then bread later in the day as a snack. But what Dad loved more than anything was Mom's bread pudding. There are many stories about Mom's bread pudding, and, to be quite honest, I am not all that sure that I will ever get the real story out of mom. The stories range from a night out drinking with friends to repeated lunches at one of her favorite New Orleans restaurants where she convinced, bribed, or even got a chef or waiter intoxicated enough to give her the recipe.

To be quite honest, I didn't love bread pudding the way the rest of our family did. I was not a fan of raisins so I would beg mom to not put them into the dessert, but she always did. I would pick each raisin out with a sense of disgust and then try to bargain with mom to pour more bourbon or rum sauce on top of mine; it never worked. Each morning after mom would bake bread pudding, Dad would cutt himself a square and pour a cup of strong, black coffee.Sitting on the couch and looking like he was in heaven he would readthe paper and become completely engrossed is a cold simple square of heaven that mom had baked.

When you decide to make this dessert/breakfast/snack, use stale bread. I often suggest to people to plan on making this yummy treat a couple of days before you actually do. I also suggest buying the bread then and the night before you

decide to bake this, put your raisins in a bowl to soak in your sauce of choice. I have been known to soak mine in brandy, bourbon or even rum.

The fun part of this recipe is once your pour the liquid mixture over the bread, use your hands and squash it all together. Squeeze over and over to make sure all of the bread is good and soaked through, and the ingredients are all thoroughly mixed together.

1 ½ loaves of STALE French bread
1 quart of milk
3 eggs
2 cups of sugar
2 or 3 tablespoons of vanilla
4 tablespoons margarine
1 cup of raisins
3 or 4 tablespoons of cinnamon- it's all about what you like

Start out by soaking raisins in brandy if you like brandy or in rum if you like rum... Break up your bread, it's best to have stale crusty bread and pour milk over bread.

Add eggs, sugar, vanilla, raisins and stir well. Pour the melted margarine in the bottom of the pan, pour in mixture and top with cinnamon. Bake in oven on 325 degrees for 35 to 45 minutes.

BAKING TIP: When you are ready to bake this dessert, place the pan with the bread pudding into a larger pan that has about one inch of water in it. Baking your dessert in water is what keeps your bread pudding moist as well as prevents the bottom of the bread pudding from burning.

BREAD PUDDING WHISKEY SAUCE

1 stick of butter
1 cup of sugar
1 egg
2 ounces of whiskey, OR bourbon, OR rum

Cook sugar and butter in a double boiler till all is dissolved. Then add well beaten egg and whip very quickly so the egg does not cook/scramble . Let mixture start to cool and add whiskey to taste and place aside until ready to serve bread pudding. Both can be refrigerated and reheated in the microwave to desired heat.

Hint: This always tastes best when you pour your own two ounces of Bourbon over ice and drink while preparing.

DAD'S FAVORITE FRUIT COOKIES

I have often been accused of being an idealist, and I don't care. There are memories of food that make me smile and then there are times that I make food that makesmore memories. Dad's fruit cookies are a sweet treat that has done both. I can remember being very excited as a child making these often seasonal cookies. These were Dad's favorite Christmas treat. I think Mom dreaded making these. It was less because of the labor and more because of the mess I would make playing with them as we made them. The other part of this was watching mom try and figure out was where to hide them after she had baked them, so Dad wouldn't eat them all. However, for days after mom baked them, Dad was having one, or two, with his cup of coffee first thing in the morning while reading the Times Picayune. Now that was my flashback. Today, when I make these cookies, I laugh because the house smells amazing and no matter who pop over,

I have to share these immediately. The best part about these cookies is that they keep for weeks if you keep them in the right container. I have been saved many a time when people "pop over." These are ready to go, and I can call them freshly baked. People LOVE these cookies.

Heck, I LOVE these cookies. The only trouble you may have is finding the candied fruit throughout the year. My solution to this has always been to stock up throughout the holidays and keep a cabinet full of the stuff so I can make these whenever I like. Now bake away and I hope 1 pound chopped dates

1 pound candied pineapple and cherries
1 pound chopped pecans
½ pound butter
1 ½ cups of sugar
2 eggs
2 ½ cups sifted flour
1 teaspoon baking soda
1 teaspoon salt
1 teaspoon vanilla

Cream butter and gradually add sugar until you have created a silky mixture. Add eggs and vanilla and continue to mix well. Sift dry ingredients with 2 cups of the flour and add to the mixture. Mix the fruit with the remaining ½ cup of flour and add to the mixture. Finally, mix in pecans and put one teaspoon of mix on an ungreased cookie sheet and bake at 350 for 15 minutes. Watch closely as they burn fast (FYI this is mom's favorite phrase when she writes a recipe for me) and let cool slightly and remove from baking sheet to cooling rack.

FIG CAKE

1 quart of canned figs or fig preserves
2 sticks of butter
2 eggs
1 ½ cups sugar
1 teaspoon baking soda
4 cups sifted flour
2 teaspoons vanilla

Mix all ingredients EXCEPT figs together and split in half. Take half of the dough and spread in a 9x13 pan, pour 1 quart of canned figs over the top. Place the rest of the dough on top and bake at 350 for 1 hour. Let cool and serve!

YUM

FOUR LAYER DELIGHT

Layer 1:

> 1 cup flour
> ½ cup pecans chopped
> ½ cup butter
> Mix and bake for 5 minutes at 350

Layer 2:

> 1 cup powdered sugar
> 1 cup cool whip
> 1- 8 ounce cream cheese softened
> Beat ingredients together and pour over first layer (cooled)

Layer 3:

> 2 packs vanilla instant pudding
> 3 cups cold milk
> Mix and pour over 2nd layer

Layer4:

> Top with remaining cool whip and sprinkle with chopped nuts if you like –
> in other words make it pretty...Chill for at least 4 hours before serving.

BANANA SPLIT PIE

2 cups graham cracker crumbs
2 Sticks of butter
2 cups of powdered sugar
1- 8 ounce cream cheese
1 can crushed pineapple (well drained)
1 container of Cool Whip
1 ½ cups of chopped pecans or walnuts
1 small jar of drained maraschino cherries

Melt 1 stick of butter and mix in graham cracker crumbs. Spread mixture in a 9x12 pan(or is a pie dish) and bake for 10 min on 350 degrees.

Cream second stick of butter, cream cheese and powdered sugar and spread on top of the baked and now cooled graham cracker crust

Add layer of sliced bananas

Add layer of crushed pineapple (drained)

Cool Whip top Layer and garnish with cherries and chopped pecans

BLACKBERRY COBBLER

It doesn't get more basic than this recipe. Simple desserts rock and often are the best dishes. Enjoy this one!

- 1 stick of butter
- 1 sup self srising flour
- 1 cup sugar
- 1 cup of milk
- 4 cups blackberries

Melt butter. Mix flour and sugar, only. Gradually add the milk and melted butter into the flour mixture. Mix well.

Put the 4 cups of blackberries in 9 x 12 glass baking dish. Pour batter over berries and bake 45 minutes. Let stand for 5 min and serve topped with decadent vanilla ice cream. Change the berries or ice cream for a different cobbler.

HOPSCOTCH COOKIES

Now for so many reasons this cookie is the sweet treat that reminds me of my brother. No matter what time of year, or where I am living or where my brother is, when I see these sweet oddly shaped pieces of dessert architecture I think of Kevin. These sweet treats tend to be party pleasers because they look unusual and your guests will try them out of pure curiosity! I think I make these throughout the year because I miss my brother or because I wish he was at an event with me. It never ceases to amaze me how a simple cookie can connect you with a loved one no matter how far away they are and no matter how long ago you shared that food memory.

½ cup peanut butter
1 can chow mien noodles
1 ½ cups marshmellows
1- 6 ounce bag butterscotch morsels
½ cup pecans

Wax paper to drop cookies on

Over low heat, combine peanut butter and butterscotch morsels blend and melt. Remove mixture from heat and gently stir in noodles and marshmellows(try not to break up your chow mein noodles too much as this is what helps to give these cookies their unique shape and size). Carefully mix by using a wooden spoon and turning ingredients together and pour in pecans before mixture gets too solidified.

Drop on wax paper by teaspoon. Let cool and store in tight container

LEMON PIE

Now here is a tempting treat that is sure to make your mouth pucker and make you reach for a cup of coffee or something to "break the richness" or "cut the sweetness" . This was another household favorite growing up. As mom or Kevin could rightfully attest to, I have ALWAYS had a sweet tooth. Mom would have to hide things in the top of the pantry at home so I would eat them. One of my favorite childhood things is in this recipe – Condensed Milk! This was better than syrup or honey or hell, even candy. This can was sweet heaven for me. Mom often used it in her hot tea, delicious. I would sneak it out of the little plastic pitcher in the fridge and spread it on bread, go and hide and sit down to enjoy every sweet bite. But THIS RECIPE – Simply Fantastic! Today I have my own Myer lemon tree in the back yard and I often use the lemons right off of my tree for this amazing dessert. It is easy and makes people who love lemon smile.

2 lemons – sometimes I add an extra half if I want my pie to be extra tart
3 eggs
 Can condensed milk
2 tablespoons flour
1 teaspoon vanilla

Grate lemon, squeeze lemon juice and separate eggs and save the whites for later. Combine and mix remaining ingredients, Add flour, vanilla, and condensed milk and stir….DO NOT USE A MIXER do this by hand!

For quick n easy use store bought pie crust bake it then add filling and bake for 5 minutes on 350 and refrigerate for 3 to 4 hours or overnight if at all possible. If you are a purist, make a pie crust and then fill bake and refrigerate.

PERFECT PETITE PECAN PIES

Now here is a recipe that I have been able to adapt over the years. Mom started out by making these for the holidays, but, today, I make the shells and put all sorts of sweet treats in them.

Shells
4 ounces of cream cheese softened
½ cup butter softened
1 cup regular flour

Combine and refrigerate for at least one hour.

Shape into 24 balls put in greased mini muffin pans and shape into shells. Bake at 350 for just about 15 minutes (watch these carefully as they burn QUICKLY).

Filling

¾ cup tightly packed brown sugar

1 teaspoon butter

1 egg

1 teaspoon vanilla

2/3 cup chopped pecans – you can add a bit more if you like

Combine ingredients, and spoon 1 teaspoon of the filling in each shell and bake again at 350 for 15 minutes.

Now if you are feeling adventurous, try different fillings including caramel, spiced apples, pineapple-basil chutney and many, many more!

M & M® COOKIES

I have been given TONS of grief for putting this in the book. BUT you must remember this cookbook is all about my life, my memories and connections to the people I LOVE. This ridiculous recipe makes me smile just to see it. We loved M & M® cookies as children. My mom will still knock an old lady down to get her Peanut M & M's®. I can remember making these for school, for Christmas and even for Easter. These cookies are FUN. I admit readily that the cookie dough for this one I eat it all. Decorating the tops of them with extra candies was my brother and I's favorite. I can remember Kevin wanting each and every cookie to look just so. There could never be too many of one color on each cookie. The candy had to be placed just so and the colors had to work to his aesthetic. I still make these cookies when I want to add a punch of color to a dessert table or I bring these cookies to someone after they are not feeling well. The bright colored candy and the fun of this cookie always makes friends smile. So go wild and mix and match whatever colors you want.

1 cup butter flavored Crisco
1 cup firmly packed brown sugar
½ cup sugar
3 teaspoons vanilla
2 eggs
2 ½ cups sifted flour
1 teaspoon baking soda
1 teaspoon salt
1 ½ cups m & m's

Blend shortening, sugars, and then beat in eggs. Sift remaining dry ingredients and then add to sugar mixture. Stir in ½ of the M & M's®. Add remaining candy to tops of cookies and then bake at 375 for 10 minutes. Remove and let cool on racks.

MILLIONAIRES

Yet another dessert that makes me smile. Nanny picked up this tradition once Maw was gone. As a child I always wanted more. This was especially true when it came to food. Nanny nicknamed me Jaws for this exact reason. I can even remember staying with Uncle Bud and Aunt Judy and eating so many cookies that I actually got sick. If there is a candy treat that I could eat until I am sick it is this one. These treats are sumptuous. I have heard people say that these are "just like turtles", but I think not! These homemade treats far surpass any option for a store bought candy and even more so many of the recipes that I have tried to make over the years that end up being nothing like this. Every year when I head back to Louisiana for Christmas I find these amazing desserts! Maw used to make them, then Nanny and Chris, and now Chris's daughter, Maddie, makes them and with each generation, they stay amazing and the love and tradition happily live on. Enjoy this wonderful candy any time of year and make whatever the event is even more special and more momentous!

- 1 can condensed milk
- 2 cups pecans
- 1- 12 ounce semi sweet chocolate chips
- 1/3 of a bar of paraffin wax

Place can of condensed milk in a full pot of water. Be sure can is covered COMPLETELY for ENTIRE TIME OR CAN WILL EXPLODE! Boil can for 3 hours ….allow water to cool and CAREFULLY remove can. Place can in refrigerator to cool and chill. Remove can 24 hours later. You now have caramel.

Melt chocolate and paraffin in double boiler. Take one teaspoon of caramel and drop into pecans to coat caramel. Now dip pecan covered ball into chocolate and then drop onto wax paper. Once candy is dry, place into sealed container and store in refrigerator.

FAMILY CARROT CAKE – OLDER GENERATION

I am laughing as I write this section of the book. If your family is as nuts about food as mine is there will always be points of contention amongst the generations when people change or adapt recipes. In my family this is one of those recipes. This is the carrot cake of the generation ahead of me. This cake is delicious. There is nothing wrong with it and I find myself making it and serving it at home, the office and even for people's birthday parties. I however have come up with an alternate recipe that I also love. I have found that many people do not like raisins or are allergic to nuts, if you are one of those people, simply omit those ingredients. Remember the recipes in this book are to be your guide. If you are a by-the-book kind of person, you need to lighten up when cooking and have some fun. Add something that you love to a recipe. After all, that is how so many of these basic foods have evolved. Now just as an FYI, you cannot leave out the basic ingredients, flour sugar eggs etc. What you can skip are things like rum (Heaven forbid), raisins, nuts etc. So my challenge to you is this, make this or any dessert and learn to make it all your own.

FAMILY CARROT CAKE – OLDER GENERATION

3 cups grated carrots
1 ½ cups of vegetable oil
2 cups of sugar
4 eggs beaten slightly
3 cups of flour
3 teaspoons baking powder
2 teaspoons baking soda
½ teaspoons salt
1 ½ teaspoons cinnamon
1 teaspoons rum
1 cup chopped nuts (pecans or walnuts)
1 cup raisins

Mix all ingredients bake in 10 inch rounds at 350 for 30 to 35 minutes

Let cool in pan 5 minutes. Let cool on baking racks 1 hour or until fully cooled until icing.

make It Yours

CREAM CHEESE ICING

Now I have a bit of a sweet tooth. I generally double all icing recipes so there is plenty of it and I do not risk running out. And by the way, who doesn't LOVE having some home-made icing in the fridge to spread on a cookie, or to easily eat with a spoon. Rob that was just for you!

1- 8 ounce cream cheese
1 stick of butter
1- 16 ounce powdered sugar
1 teaspoon of rum – of course
1 teaspoon of vanilla

Soften cream cheese and butter. In large bowl pour in rum and vanilla. Set mixer to medium and start mixing. Slowly add powdered sugar until you have a light and fluffy mixture and then ice your cake and ENJOY!!!

MAW MAW'S PRALINES

Now these are not your typical pralines......these are Maw Maw's! These are pure Cajun candy love. I alwaysthink of Maw when these are around. I never saw these made. I would get to Maw's and they were magically there. I can honestly say I never made these until I was about 30! It was trying to get past the magic of these sweets. I have learned that these are not difficult to make you simply have to pay attention to what you are doing and these will come out just perfectly.

> 1 cup sugar
> 1 cup brown sugar
> ¾ cup evaporated milk
> ¼ pound butter
> 1 tablespoon vanilla
> Pecan halves

Combine sugars and evaporated milk in a pot and dissolve completely on medium heat. Bring to a boil and stir frequently for about 2 - 3 minutes.

Remove from heat and add butter and vanilla. Now stir in pecans. Mix briskly for about 2 minutes and then spoon mixture out onto wax paper.

Hint – I often put newspaper underneath my wax paper to prevent any grease or seeping liquid from getting onto my countertop.

AUNT ANNIE'S RED VELVET CAKE

½ cup shortening
1 ½ cup sugar
2 eggs
2 teaspoons cocoa
2 or 2 ½ teaspoons red food coloring
1 teaspoon salt
1 teaspoon vanilla
1 cup buttermilk
2 ½ cups sifted flour
1 teaspoon baking soda
1 tablespoon vinegar

Cream sugar and shortening until fluffy. Add eggs one at a time beating after each one. Mix cocoa with food coloring until it looks like a paste and then add the salt. Add red mixture to sugar mixture. Combine vanilla and buttermilk. Now alternate between buttermilk and flour adding each to sugar mixture. Finally combine soda and vinegar and slowly STIR, not beat, to mixture.

Pour batter into three 8 or 9 inch greased and floured round pans. Bake at 350 for 25 to 30 minutes.

Now the best part – Frosting

16 ounces of powdered sugar
1 stick of butter
1- 8 ounce cream cheese softened
2 ½ teaspoons vanilla
½ cup chopped pecans – Optional
Beat all together and frost cake once it has cooled.

MAW MAW'S OATMEAL COOKIES

Whether or not it was Uncle Bud, Uncle John, Uncle Pat, Uncle Ronnie or Dad these were the favorite of the Uncles. Uncle John used to tease Maw that he knew we were coming for a visit because Maw would bake these and tell Uncle John they were for Bill. Of course he was allowed to have a couple. Maw loved to make everyone feel special, important, and loved. She did this through the food she made. No matter whom it was in our very large family, she knew what everyone's favorite dish or dessert was. She oftentimes went out of her way to make it special for whoever it was. These cookies were always a hit. They were made with love and it became more and more difficult for Maw to make them as her arthritis and osteoporosis got worse. She was a trooper though, and she forged ahead because she wanted each and every one of us to know just how special we were to her. I don't think any of us didn't realize just how much Maw loved us and just how much she loved to show us through her simple yet ever so special food that she prepared for us. These cookies were a year rounder for us. There was never a special occasion or a holiday needed for these. They were simply there in the big oval tins that depicted painted scenes upon them. Those cookies just waited for us. It was always magic to open those tins or the orange cookie jar to see which of her two most famous cookies awaited us. I could always tell which one held these oatmeal cookies because I could watch and see which one of my uncles all gravitated towards.

1 cup of shortening
1 cup of brown sugar
1 cup sugar
2 well beaten eggs
1 tablespoon vanilla
1 ½ cups flour
1 teaspoon salt
1 teaspoons baking soda
3 cups of quick cooking oats
½ cup chopped pecans

Thoroughly cream shortening and sugar. Then add eggs and vanilla and beat well. Sift all dry ingredients and add to the creamed mixture and finally add oats and nuts and mix well. Shape these into rolls and wrap in plastic wrap and chill or freeze.

Slice in about ¼ inch thick and place on ungreased pan and bake at 350 for 10 minutes. Let cool on cooling rack.

HINT: These can be frozen as a roll for quite a while and then taken out cut, baked and enjoyed on a moment's notice!

Your Ideas

PEANUT BUTTER BALLS

2 cups honey
3 cups creamy peanut butter
5 cups nonfat dry milk
6 cups quick cooking oats

Line 2 baking sheets with waxed paper. Set aside.

In a large bowl, combine honey, peanut butter, dry milk and oats. Mix with an electric mixer until dough is too stiff to mix. Mix with your hands until dough is smooth and well combined. Using your hands, shape mixture into 1 1/2 inch balls. Place on prepared pans and freeze until hard.

Store in freezer in resealable plastic bags for up to 2 months. Makes 10 dozen.

OLD FASHIONED TEA CAKES

This is your family standard "decorate and ice me" cookie. Cut out whatever shape you desire and decorate away. I used to love colored sugars for these to create Christmas cookies, Easter eggs, and even flags for holiday cookies made from scratch. So be creative and know you can make whatever shape you like and just go for it. It's all a Whole Heap of FUN!

1 cup of butter
2 cups of sugar
3 eggs
2 tablespoons of buttermilk
5 cups of all purpose flour
1 teaspoon baking soda
1 teaspoon vanilla or 2 if you like vanilla

Cream butter and add sugar gradually beating well. Add eggs one at a time beating well after each one. Add buttermilk and beat again. Combine the flour and soda and slowly add to mixture. Finally add the vanilla. Cover and place mixture in metal bowl into refrigerator overnight.

On a lightly floured surface, Roll dough out to about ¼ inch thick and cut out with cookie cutters or desired shapes. Place on a lightly greased cookie sheet about an inch apart and sprinkle with sugar and bake on 400 for 7 to 8 minutes. Watch these closely as then burn fast. Remove and place on rack to cool.

PECAN PIE

Now in the South, pecan pie is a staple. Pecan pie can be as diverse as the people who live throughout the South. Everyone has their grandma or their great aunt's recipe. I think I have made about 40 different types and varieties of pecan pie. I would VERY STRONGLY suggest that you approh pecan pie as something you make your own. Below is what I often use as my basic pie. I have added chocolate, caramel, peppermint, condensed milk and bourbon to this basic pie. So get to experimenting and make this pie A Whole Heap your own!

1 cup Karo Corn syrup
3 slightly beaten eggs
1/8 teaspoon vanilla
1 cup sugar
2 tablespoons butter meted
1 cup pecan halves
1 uncooked 9 inch pastry shell

Mix all ingredients. Preheat oven to 400 and bake pie shell and filling for for 15 minutes. Reduce oven temperature to 350 and bake an additional 30 to 35 minutes. You know your pie is ready when the edges are set and firm and the center is slightly soft.

SUGAR AND CINNAMON PECANS

4 cups of pecan halves
½ cup butter
3 egg whites
½ teaspoon salt
¾ cup sugar
1 ½ teaspoon cinnamon

Spread nuts on a shallow baking pan and bake for 25 minutes on 250 degrees. Remove from oven and pour into bowl. Pour butter on the hot baking sheet and tilt till it melts and coats. Pour nuts back into pan and us wooden spoon to spread across pan and butter. Set aside while preparing the coating

Turn oven up to 300 degrees.

Beat egg whites in a separate bowl until foamy. Add salt, sugar and cinnamon slowly and while continually beating. Beat until you have stiff white puffs beginning to form. Now pout mixture over nuts on pan and spread with your wooden spoon.

Place pan back into oven at 300 degrees for 35 to 40 minutes watching closely and stir till nuts appear dry. Let cool and serve!

HOLY BOATS IT'S A RUM CAKE

Let's face it people.....I like rum and I like cake.....so the two of them together is HEAVEN! This recipe is SUPER EASY and this cake will keep for a solid week or so if you keep it under a dome. And trust me; there is only 1 cake better than this one with a cup of coffee in the morning. This cake is the one I tend to make for raffles, receptions or charity lunches at the house. This cake is always a hit. I remember the first time I had this cake. Mom had made it as an experiment before agreeing to bring it to Thanksgiving. I think Mom, Dad, Kevin and I ate most of the cake that night. I also remember the guilty look on Dad's face the next morning as he had an empty plate and half a cup of coffee with him. It goes without saying that the cake was a complete hit that year at Thanksgiving and has since become a household standard of ours. There are several ways to mix it up with this delicious cake and it is so very easy to be creative so use your imagination and make a Whole Heap of deliciousness.

1 cup of chopped pecans
1 yellow cake mix
1 vanilla instant pudding mix
4 eggs
½ cup water
½ cup vegetable or canola oil
½ cup dark rum

Grease and flour bunt pan, put chopped pecans on the bottom.

Mix all remaining ingredients together and beat well. Pour mixture over pecans. Bake at 325 for 1 hour. Let cool for 5 minutes and remove from pan. Use toothpicks or small wooden skewers and poke holes in the top of the cake so it will better absorb the glaze.

Rum glaze for cake

- ¼ cup of butter
- ¼ cup water
- 1 cup sugar
- ½ cup dark rum

Melt butter in pot and stir in sugar and water. Boil for 5 minutes stirring entire time. Remove from heat and add rum. Let cool for 3 minutes and brush onto cake.

Options: Make this your own by trying things like zest a fresh lemon into your glaze and a bit more atop the cake. I have also used oranges and I have tried using different types of fruit to add changes to the look of the overall cake. Several times I have added cinnamon to the glaze and atop the cake for a new twist on this old family favorite. I can't wait to hear your own attempts at making it your own.

Pecan Tarts

I laugh at how my taste in food changes over time. I couldn't stand eating these as a kid, but I loved making these! These desserts were not quite sweet enough. These days, I LOVE these. They are just the perfect way to end a very rich meal. These delicious treats also keep well for a couple of weeks, not that I have ever been able to keep any for that long.

2 sticks of butter
8 tablespoons powdered sugar
1 teaspoon vanilla
2 cups of pecans chopped
2 cups flour

Cream butter powdered sugar and vanilla. Gradually add flour, dough will be stiff. Now add pecans and blend through by squeezing dough with your hands and roll into small balls and place on a cookie sheet.

Bake 15 to 20 minutes at 350 degrees. After cooled pour powdered sugar into a bowl and roll balls in powdered sugar. Serve or store.

Simple Quick Cheesecake

¼ cup butter
1 cup graham cracker crumbs
¼ cup sugar
2- 8 ounce packages of cream cheese softened
1 can condensed milk
3 eggs
¼ teaspoon salt
¼ cup lemon juice
1- 8 ounce container of sour cream
Preheat oven to 300

Combine butter, crumbs and sugar and pack firmly in 9 inch pan. In a large mixing bowl, beat the cream cheese till fluffy and then beat in eggs one at a time. Then add milk and salt and beat until smooth. Stir in the lemon juice. Pour mixture into the pan and bake for 50 to 55 minutes. Cool completely then add sour cream to top and refrigerate.

STRAWBERRIES

The Sweetest Things

Louisiana has many treasures and one of my favorites is the strawberry crop that comes out of Ponchatula. There are many of you out there who grew up in areas where strawberries are grown locally or a wonderful summer plant on the patio. Where I grew up, there was nothing more exciting than the anticipation for the arrival of the sweet summer crop that magically appeared on the side of a road in the back of a pickup truck. The magically sweet fruit would lead to delicious desserts created by mom and frequently topped everything from warm pancakes or a bowl of cereal to ice cream or home-made angel food or pound cake. The following couple of pages are some fresh sweet ways to play with this fantastic fruit. If you aren't up for the challenge wash 'em slice 'em and throw some sugar in, refrigerate and spoon over cake or eat 'em up!!!

STRAWBERRIES JAMAICA

- 4 ounces cream cheese
- ½ cup firmly packed brown sugar
- 1 ½ cups sour cream
- 2 tablespoons of Gran Mariner
- 1 quart of fresh strawberries

Beat cream cheese with hand mixer on medium until smooth. Add sugar, sour cream, and Grand Mariner and beat for an additional 1 minute or until smooth. Cover and chill serve as a dip to the fresh strawberries.

Hint – I have been known to finely chop fresh strawberries and beat them into this mixture for a little extra flair.

STRAWBERRY CAKE

Ok I confess this was one of my summer favorites.......Boy is this one simple too

- 1 box of white cake mix
- ½ cup oil
- ½ cup water
- ½ cup of frozen strawberries
- 4 egg Whites

Mix together and bake at 350 for 25 to 30 minutes in a greased and floured pan.

Frosting

- 16 ounces of confectioner sugar
- 1 stick butter softened
- ½ cup strawberries

Cream together on high speed until stiff and smooth

QUICKIE STRAWBERRY PIE

- 1 small box strawberry Jell-O
- 3 teaspoons cornstarch
- 1 cup of cold water
- 1- 16 ounce frozen sliced strawberries

Boil everything except strawberries and mix well. Let cool. and Once cooled add strawberries and then pour mixture into a baked pie shell. Cover in whipped cream and garnish with fresh strawberries and refrigerate.

CREAMY STRAWBERRY PIE

- 8 ounces of cream cheese softened
- 1 can of condensed milk
- 2 ½ cups of mashed strawberries
- 2 tablespoons of lemon juice
- 1 container of cool whip

Beat cream cheese until smooth, add remaining ingredients and pour into a cooked and cooled pie shell. Chill and serve.

Hint – This entire pie can even be frozen and served later. Talk about convenient.

MAW'S OLD-FASHIONED SUGAR COOKIES

Here it is, the other Maw Classic Cookie!!! This was the other cookie everyone looked for and expected when going over to Maw's. There always seemed to be an endless stream of these sweet treats in addition to Maw's oatmeal cookies. I loved these cookies. I still make these as often as possible to keep on hand around the house. These cookies are a simple cookie that I have done so many things with. I have iced them with frosting, I have sprinkled them with sugar, I have even topped each one with a small piece of dried fruit. Maw's favorite thing to do with these cookies was to place a half of a maraschino cherry dead center of each cookie. I can remember asking her once why she did this. Her response was simple and has become the heart of the A Whole Heap. "Well baby it makes each one pretty and a little more special."

So no matter what the occasion, there is nothing that can make me smile like a special little sugar cookie. So get baking and make a moment momentous for someone you love. Like the oatmeal cookies, these sugar cookies are amazing with your cup of coffee or a glass of ice cold milk!

> 2/3 cup shortening
> 1 teaspoon vanilla
> 1 egg
> 4 teaspoon of milk
> 2 cups all purpose flour sifted
> 1 ½ teaspoons baking powder
> ¼ teaspoon salt

Thoroughly cream shortening sugar and vanilla. Add eggs one at a time and beat until fluffy. Stir in milk and now begin to sift in dry ingredients and blend into the cream mixture. Divide dough in half. Chill for at least 2 hours. On a lightly floured surface roll dough out into 1/8" thick. Cut out with cookie cutter or even a water glass. Bake on a greased cookie sheet at 375 for 6 to 7 minutes. Watch these closely as they turn fast. Cool on a rack. And think of my maw maw.

VANILLA WAFER CAKE

1 cup of butter
1 cup of sugar
6 eggs
½ cup milk
1 7 ounce pack of flaked coconut
1 cup chopped pecans
1- 12 ounce box of vanilla wafers crushed

Cream butter and add sugar and beat until smooth. Add eggs one at a time beating well after each one. Add crushed vanilla wafers alternating with the milk. Finally add coconut and pecans. Pour batter into a greased and floured bunt pan and bake at 275 for about 80 to 90 minutes.

Make It Yours

FAST AND EASY CHEESECAKE

When in a pinch, this will do......otherwise you can do better!

2 8 ounce cream cheese
2 eggs
¾ cup sugar
1 tablespoon lemon juice
1 ½ teaspoon vanilla
Soften cream cheese and mix ingredients in above order

Place paper cups in muffin tin and put 1 vanilla wafer in the bottom of each. Pour mixture in and bake at 300 degrees for 20 to 22 minutes watching carefully. Cool and top with whatever your lil heart desires.

AMARETTO

2 cups sugar
2 cups water
Skin of one large lemon
Add 6 teaspoons of almond extract
2 teaspoons vanilla extract
1 teaspoon chocolate extract
2 and 2/3 cups of vodka
1 drop of green food coloring
4 drops of yellow food coloring
3 drops of red food coloring

Boil sugar water and lemon rind. After all sugar is dissolved and liquid is at a rolling boil turn off. Remove from heat and let cool completely. After liquid is fully cooled add remainig ingredients and then remove lemon rind. Store in a tightly sealed container.

DRAMBUIE

2 cups of water
3 cups of sugar
Skin of 1 lemon
Add 5 1/3 cups of scotch
1 drop green food coloring
4 drops of yellow food coloring
3 drops of red food coloring

Boil sugar water and lemon rind. After all sugar is dissolved and liquid is at a rolling boil turn off. Remove from heat and let cool completely. After liquid is fully cooled add remainig ingredients and then remove lemon rind and add 1 teaspoon of vanilla. Store in a tightly sealed container.

Appendix

Your Ideas